BEYOND F
Vision,
Hope and Generosity

BEYOND FEAR
Vision,
Hope and Generosity

The 'After Socialism?' Group
(CENTRE FOR THEOLOGY & PUBLIC ISSUES)
EDITOR: ANDREW R MORTON

SAINT ANDREW PRESS

First published in 1998 by
SAINT ANDREW PRESS
121 George Street, Edinburgh EH2 4YN

on behalf of the 'After Socialism?' Group,
CENTRE for THEOLOGY and PUBLIC ISSUES

ISBN 0 7152 0759 8

British Library Cataloguing in Publication Data
A catalogue record for this book
is available from the British Library.

ISBN 0715207598

Cover and **design concept** by Mark Blackadder.
Cover photograph © Image Bank/Bryan Haynes.
Typeset in 11/12 pt Bembo.
Printed and **bound** by Bell and Bain, Glasgow.

CONTENTS

✳

CONTENTS

FOREWORD

✳

by The 'After Socialism?' Group

THIS book, *Beyond Fear: Vision, Hope and Generosity*, was completed in the month and almost to the day – 1 May 1997 – when the British electorate chose a new Parliament, which produced a new government, led by a new Prime Minister, who claims to stand in both the socialist and the Christian traditions and who holds out a promise of a new Britain.

The book examines these two traditions – socialist and Christian – and while it is critical of them, it comes to the conclusion that both are alive and both have an important contribution to make to the future of this country, as of others. But the book is not an attempt to recruit adherents to either of these traditions, nor yet an exercise in articulating or justifying a new consensus or new prospectus. It tries to do something deeper and more radical. It explores the very nature of hope and vision, and of what makes the new really new – and it sees an inextricable connection between the personal and the political realms. In this sense, it is about a new kind of politics, not a new programme, far less a new party, but a new way of doing politics and of being political, which involves transcending fear, forming vision, acting hope and structuring generosity.

The book grew out of the work of a group of people called together by the Centre for Theology and Public Issues in the University of Edinburgh following a conference in 1994 on 'After Socialism? The Future of Radical Christianity'. The proceedings of this conference were published by the Centre, under the same title, as its Occasional Paper No. 31.

The core of the group met regularly for over two years and others contributed through more occasional participation. Five people were the co-authors of the book itself: Professor Zenon Bankowski of the Centre for Law and Society in the University of Edinburgh, Mr Stephen Baron of the Department of Education in the University of Glasgow, the Rev. Dr Graham Blount, minister of Old and St Modan's Parish Church in Falkirk and Honorary

Secretary of the Church of Scotland Committee on Church and Nation, Mr John Hughes, former Principal of Ruskin College, Oxford and the Rev. Dr Andrew Morton, Associate Director of the Centre for Theology and Public Issues, who convened the group. For parts of the text they drew heavily on material contributed by two others: Ms Isobel Lindsay of the Department of Government in the University of Strathclyde and the Rev. Professor Duncan Forrester, Dean of the Faculty of Divinity and Professor of Christian Ethics and Practical Theology in the University of Edinburgh.

Others who made a more general contribution were: Dr Marcella Althaus-Reid, Mr Rab Burnett, Mr Stuart Holden, Dr Mike McCabe, and Rev. George Wilkie.

Finally, the process took account of the contributions made at the 1994 conference by Professor Charles Davis, Emeritus Professor of Religion in Concordia University, Montreal, Professor David McLellan, Professor of Political Theory in the University of Kent, Mr Ian Wood, Lecturer in History in Napier University, Canon Paul Oestreicher, Director of the International Ministry of Coventry Cathedral, Professor Alistair Kee, Professor of Religious Studies in the University of Edinburgh, Ms Kay Carmichael, former Lecturer in Social Administration and Social Work in the University of Glasgow, and Professor Jan Milic Lochman, Emeritus Professor of Dogmatics in the University of Basel.

The nature of the process which led to the book, including the composition of the group which produced it, is noteworthy. It was essentially a collective activity, involving sustained conversations from which emerged a common mind. The diversity of the group was a necessary feature, both in its interdisciplinary diversity and what might be called its *intercredal* variety. The disciplines of sociology, economics, political science, law, pedagogy, theology and philosophy were represented. No less important was the representation of different degrees of adherence and non-adherence to both the Christian tradition and the socialist tradition; the writing did not presuppose either an adherence to Christianity or a commitment to socialism.

The approach of the book could be described as 'non-dogmatic' in two senses. First, it is more methodological than substantive, in the sense that it suggests a way of relating theological discourse and political discourse to one another rather than offering a specific policy prospectus. Second, it is a theologically and historically informed interpretation of present social reality in this part of the

world rather than a systematic set of timeless theological propositions. This approach is not simply a reflection of the composition
of the group; it is what the authors judged to be needed at this
historical juncture. They believe that three things about the present
social context show the need for that to which this book aspires.

The first, which was the original impetus, was and is a deep
dissatisfaction with prevailing interpretations of the outcome of
developments in the 1980s and of the great changes in Europe
around 1990. This is elaborated in the Introduction, in what is said
there about the 'Post-Age'.

The second development which makes the aim of this book
timely is the growing interest in the relevance of Christian
theology to political activity in general and to current political
prospectuses in particular. This interest is most recently evidenced
by the attention given to the Roman Catholic Bishops of England
and Wales' publication *The Common Good*, to the Council of
Churches for Britain and Ireland's publication *Unemployment and
the Future of Work,* to such books as *Reclaiming the Ground* and *God
in the Market Place,* and indeed to the continuing reverberations
from Baroness (then Mrs) Thatcher's address to the Church of
Scotland General Assembly in 1988, the so-called 'Sermon on the
Mound'.

The third development, which has now supervened, is the
emphasis on newness on the part of the new government of the
United Kingdom, together with the associated prospect of a very
new Parliament in Scotland.

The reference to Scotland prompts the rather obvious observation that this book emanates from Scotland. However, the society
which it concerns and to which it is addressed is as wide as, indeed
wider than, Britain. Naturally the experience of the group is coloured
by its mainly Scottish location and some of the illustrative material
reflects this. It may also be that the recent Scottish sense of political
marginalisation in the United Kingdom gives an added value to its
perspective; for, as will become evident, the book sees merit in 'the
view from the margins'.

One regret of the authors is that they did not succeed in listening as much as they originally intended to those whom they regard
as important co-authors, the 'silent majority'. A listening exercise
in Easterhouse in Glasgow, which is reflected in the book, was to
have been one of many. However, several of the authors brought
with them a history of involvement in such listening and of participation in relevant projects over many years.

Finally, this book is offered to a general readership. While it may find the most ready audience among people in political parties, among the so-called 'educated laity' (and clergy) of the churches, and among those in higher education courses in theology, political science, social policy, law and the like, the authors' conviction is that its subject matter is relevant to the many and not only the few. For its message is about a transformation of the citizenship of all.

Zenon Bankowski
Stephen Baron
Graham Blount
John Hughes
Andrew Morton

PART ONE

Pre-Vision in a Post-Age

INTRODUCTION

✳

THIS book has two important features: it is post-1990 and it is about hope.

Post-1990

Developments in the 1980s and watershed events around 1990 seemed to bequeath to the 1990s a changed world. Future historians may see things differently; but rightly or wrongly there was a widespread perception in the early 1990s that the world had significantly changed. In what way?

1990 and its antecedents meant for many 'the end of socialism', the focal event being the collapse of 'realsocialism' in central and east Europe and above all in the Soviet Union.

It goes without saying that reactions to that event were various. Doubtless there were some cautious and less vocal observers who played down the challenges, believing that while everything changes, everything remains the same. Undoubtedly also there were socialists who saw the demise of 'realsocialism' as the end not of socialism but of 'unreal' socialism, a Leninist-Stalinist impostor, or alternatively regarded it as the end of a schism within socialism. However, very many regarded what had happened, not only in the eastern bloc but also in the west including in the United Kingdom and possibly around the world, as a major change and one which could be characterised as 'the end of socialism'.

There was, however, a sharp division between those who rejoiced and those who mourned over this change; some sighed with relief and others with sorrow.

The rejoicers were glad for two types of reason. They, or at least some of them, disagreed with the socialist approach and were obviously pleased at what they saw as its failure to work, to win allegiance, to survive. But they, or some of them, also rejoiced at something more far-reaching, namely what Fukuyama called 'the end of history'; this meant that humanity had arrived at the end-time, and what had triumphed in the end was not socialism or any other such utopian approach, but liberal democratic capitalism, to which there was now no alternative.

The mourners were sad also for two types of reason. They, or some of them, agreed with the socialist approach and were obviously saddened at what they saw as its failure; but they, or some of them, also grieved over something more far-reaching, namely their very different interpretation of 'the end of history'; this phrase meant for them, not the arrival of the end-time, but the end of the optimistic view of history as culminating in an end-time, a view which had inspired the Enlightenment, the romantics and the various radical movements, democratic, republican, liberal and socialist, which had dominated much eighteenth, nineteenth and twentieth century social theory and practice.

The group which presents this study and the conference in 1994 out of which the group grew were a response to this post-1990 situation. The response was prompted partly by the obvious thought that such a major change in the world or at least in many people's perception of it merited closer examination; but it was prompted even more by a grave unease over the reactions to it, both the mourners' and the rejoicers'. Had socialism really died? Was the new post-historical and post-socialist order really so wonderful and was there really no alternative to it? There was a longing for a better alternative but none seemed on offer; although criticisms of the now prevailing 'order' or modifications of it were being voiced, no clear alternatives to it were being offered.

When the group began to get to grips with this matter, it uncovered what it came to see as a central issue within it, namely the nature of hope.

Hope

The group saw, as a main and highly determinative feature of the contemporary situation, the absence of hope. It may need little argument that this was true of the 'mourners'; but the group came to believe that it was also true of the 'rejoicers'.

For the mourners, as already implied, there were two deaths in one: more particularly the death of socialism and more generally the death of the basically optimistic view of history. Without 'history', the movement towards a better future, and without 'socialism', giving content to that movement, there was a big bereavement. So this was not just the collapse of one source of hope and its replacement by another, but the total collapse of hope, which left a vacuum.

Although on the face of it the rejoicers *were* hopeful, being pleased with the triumph of liberal democratic capitalism, the group came to believe that they too lacked hope. There is of course the obvious sense in which those who believe that humanity has arrived do not need hope. However, the group came to see the rejoicers as in a more profound sense devoid of hope. The analysis of the nature of hope in the following study will show why.

Other factors, in addition to the 'end of socialism', also contributed to the sense of hopelessness in Britain. For some time the end of empire and of world power status had had a dispiriting nostalgic effect. Then in the 1980s the undoing by the Thatcherite New Right of the post-war social democratic consensus had undermined the hopes of those who belonged to that consensus and had assumed its permanence. In Scotland there was a further undermining of hope through the perceived undoing of its distinctive institutions and ethos by an authoritarian and foreign-seeming government and the associated 'doomsday' denial of aspirations for self-government. Then in the 1990s were added throughout Europe the failure of expectations of a new dawn of peace and peace dividend after the end of the Cold War — the morning after the first euphoric intoxication.

All of this meant the absence of a coherent framework of aspiration and of values, leaving a moral vacuum. The danger of this ethical fragmentation had been made evident in Britain in the 1980s when selfishness became virtue. The vacuum was not being filled by the two social philosophies which alone appeared to offer an alternative to the dominant one; for both the vague liberalism which had been around for a long time and the no less vague communitarianism which was arriving on the scene lacked a coherently articulated hope. There was an altogether dispiriting absence of any genuinely alternative aspiration that had the necessary combination of imaginative freshness and articulated coherence.

In particular, one looked in vain to the 'Left intellectuals'; they were strangely silent. It is now clear that they were at a loss and in disarray because they were thrown by Thatcherism. Previously their picture of things was that the British consensus, which had been dominant since the Second World War and involved the welfare state and the mixed economy, was a form of capitalism, not 'red in tooth and claw' but tamed; their task was to challenge it and to show the way beyond it towards more socialist forms; and their attempt to think through this socialism generated great intellectual ferment, becoming almost the intellectual orthodoxy. Then came Thatcherism, which took over not only the political but also the intellectual leadership. It threw them, by reversing the picture entirely. Following Hayek and others, it regarded the post-war consensus not as tamed *capitalism* but as tamed *socialism,* and accordingly sought to move the country away from it towards 'true' capitalism. The Left intellectual field went into crisis and fragmentation; and so no fresh and coherent alternative was forthcoming from there.

It will be argued in this book that neither picture of the post-war consensus is helpful, that all such dominating consensuses are dangerous in any case, and that linking market and welfare, though necessary, does not entail a return to that old consensus. However, the point here is that the particular uncreativeness of the intellectual Left and the general absence of a coherent framework of alternative aspiration was the context in which this study was undertaken and which led it to examine more closely the nature of hope and of vision and their bearing on the political future.

While the study has a particular focus on the British context, the issues are general human ones. Since the events which triggered the study and the people who engaged in it were largely European, it may well suffer from a degree of Eurocentrism. Whether it does or not, it needs to be seen as one small contribution from one country to a debate which must be worldwide.

As the study progressed it threw up six propositions which it then explored. They are:

1. that hope is essential to human existence, both personal and social;

2. that the view of history as a progression to a better end-time, which has so shaped modern social philosophies including socialism, is seriously defective and a misunderstanding of hope; but

3. that socialism is a living tradition capable of contributing to the transformative vision which belongs to hope, and that reports of its death, like that of Mark Twain, are 'greatly exaggerated';

4. that Christianity, which is also a living tradition, is a powerful source both of understanding and of the generation of hope and its associated vision;

5. that creative interaction between these two traditions, which there has been in the past, should continue in the future and is likely to be a fruitful creator of the transformative vision, in the absence of which the people are perishing; and

6. that a key concept giving substance to hope and shape to vision is 'structured generosity'.

CHAPTER 1

*From Fear
to Hope*

The Fear of Hope

ON 9 October 1995 there was a short piece in *The Scotsman*
(page 11) by Iain MacWhirter on the growing trend of intro-
ducing religion into politics, something which he thought had had
its day. Apart from the 'culture shock to cynical old hacks like me'
what he thought problematic was:

> I can appreciate that there is a spiritual dimension to life, but I don't
> think that it should play too much of a role in politics, which is a sordid
> but necessary world of compromise and moral ambiguity. Governments
> need managers and not ministers; policy not sermons. And vicars should
> stick to the pulpit.

Obviously by this he was not meaning to say that churches have
not got their 'hands dirty' and have always, in a pure manner, kept
away – clearly, to their cost, they have not. Rather what he seemed
to imply was that the sort of ethics that the churches espouse in
theory is not really suitable for the dirty, practical business that is
politics: one version of 'render unto Caesar what is Caesar's'.

St Augustine is frequently claimed as the classic source of this
position in Christianity – the two cities of God and of the World
cannot mix. Religious hope can be, and often is, individualised and
made so private that it has no obvious public bearing. When, in
her 'Sermon on the Mound', Mrs Thatcher quoted from that
strangely chauvinist hymn 'I vow to thee, my country', she concentrated on the verse about 'another country, I've heard of long
ago' which grows 'soul by soul and silently' and whose 'ways are
ways of gentleness and all her ways are peace'. It is for this other
country, she suggested, that we should hope, and such hope has little
bearing on what goes on in the earthly country, to which the singer
vows 'the service of my love', 'the love that makes undaunted the
final sacrifice'.

This position has, to be fair, a respectable theological ancestry, stretching back through Luther's Two Kingdoms theory to a certain interpretation of St Augustine. However, this interpretation of St Augustine is contested. Moreover, whether it is indeed congruent with the biblical witness we would doubt, and whether it is capable of engaging effectively with false and diabolic hopes seems unlikely. Edwyn Bevan presented it in one of the preparatory volumes for the 1938 Oxford Conference on 'Church, Community and State'. In the true Christian outlook, he wrote, there is no earthly goal in view. The human trajectory goes across the line of earthly history seeking a goal in the unseen world. This world is simply a platform to be crossed between birth and death, until people enter 'individual by individual', into the unseen world, the world always there beside the visible one. The creation of the Divine Community in that invisible world is the 'supreme hope', before which all earthly hopes pale into insignificance, as 'everything that happens on this temporal platform, now or in the future, is of minor importance'. 'Whenever the main stress is laid upon 'building Jerusalem in England's green and pleasant land,' he concludes, 'the Christian attitude to the world is abandoned.'[1]

Accounts of the Christian hope may thus be seen to vary from the baptism of some secular political cause, so that no distinction is seen between the Nazareth manifesto of Jesus and the Internationale, to a private, escapist and alienating hope which has nothing to say to secular hopes except to deny their validity totally.

But it is not with the classical Two Kingdoms position that we are mainly concerned here. Rather, MacWhirter's attack can tell us a lot about the present state of political life and political reality in this country. For what is going on in MacWhirter's piece is not really that classical debate; rather it manifests a fear.

What is feared, and what is done, and can be done, about it, is what we are concerned with here. What is feared? Put baldly, what is feared is the transformative power of hope as manifested in a new social vision. We do not want talk of values to reach in and disturb the comfortable world that we have fashioned for ourselves; to be disturbed in our self-referential circles where we hear only what we want to hear; where we are blind to, and afraid of, anything that threatens to shatter our cosy world. In looking at the world of politics, for example, one will not, with a recent exception to which we will return, find much about values, what ought to be done and what it is right to do. Rather we see descriptions of what politicians are doing and what effect that will have on the power plays in which various, if not all of them, indulge. What counts as politics and is so reported is what happens in Parliament and the other seats of power and decision making and what impact that will have on the possibility of one side or the other gaining power. We can say then that politics has become concerned not with what it is right to do but with how what is done will, since we live in a democracy, gain votes for the propagators of it at the next elections. 'We need managers not ministers, policies not sermons.' Politics is the preserve of professional politicians; we talk of 'the political class' and that, of course, includes those who symbiotically live with it and write about it. Politics is what that group does and is to be judged, and attacked, in those terms. Politics is a system about getting votes. And so when anything shatters that cosy self-referentiality, there is a horrified reaction and an attempt to negate it.

Now we are not wanting to say that it is a fear of the power of the Christian message that prompts this attack. Rather it is the fear of an injection of values from the outside, as it were. And why is this? Because we have lost the hope that there is anything that can transform the world and our lives. We seek refuge in realism and are afraid of endangering what we have. That is then why communitarianism, a theory which seems to have been espoused by the new Labour Party, is rubbished as being Christian ethics in disguise. At least then it can be seen as something outside and necessarily so. But there is more to this attack as well. For it projects on the values – the vision – that fear as well. In setting it up the way that MacWhirter did, what we see is the idea that those who have this vision of values should fear those values being contaminated as well – that they should stay aloof but not get involved, perhaps guide but at a distance and not risk their purity by wading into that murky sea of politics. This seems to us to be false and entirely missing the awesome message of the crucifixion.

The Christian Hope

Hopes are, of course, of many kinds. Some are an escape from reality, pipe-dreams or expressions of alienation. Some are strictly individual and private. Other hopes of a political sort have shown this century how hope as the search for utopia can become appalling tyranny. Other hopes have generated great and humane movements for reform and for liberation. Many, but not all, forms of hope are rooted, at least at their birth, in religious ground.

Religion tends to generate 'a total hope', an orientation towards the future which is not partial or limited, but all-encompassing. The Judaeo-Christian tradition in particular appears to have had down the centuries a particularly close link with utopian hopes, and an expectancy about the future. Indeed one can say that the linked themes of eschatology, promise and the future are central and indispensable elements in this tradition. Here, faith gives substance to hope, shapes and sustains hope; faith and hope are inseparably linked together.

This hope is at its heart and throughout social. The principal images used for the future are not those of the flight of the alone to the Alone, or the soul's ascent to God, but the powerful symbols of the Reign of God for the coming of which we pray, the City that believers seek whose builder and maker is God, the New Jerusalem, that comes down out of heaven from God. These images all suggest a coming just ordering of relationships; in hope we look forward to the future triumph of righteousness and justice. The hope also has judgement at its heart; there is here no evasion of the gravity of sin and offence, oppression and injustice. In the City, in the New Jerusalem, justice will be enthroned. In judgement the poor and the weak are to be vindicated and upheld. This hope challenges the existing orders of injustice, violence and brutality. The hope is good news to the poor, and all who suffer.

Believers hope for something that will be given; they do not construct the City themselves. Blake's words, 'till we have built Jerusalem', strike a distinctively modern and activist note. But we are enjoined to pray for the coming of the Reign of God, and to seek the Kingdom and its justice above all other things. We are to prepare for the coming of God's new order of which we already have a foretaste in the Jesus-event and in the life and worship of the Church. And believers should also seek to discern the seeds of the Kingdom in the life of the world, and nurture them there.

Such social hopes are in practice forms of protest against the existing situation with its inbuilt injustice; they present, often in an elaborate code of imagery, an alternative reality; they refuse to make absolute present structures; they present an open future, full of possibilities; and thus they can motivate and sustain great movements of change. They can support people through times of oppression and suffering, and enable them to struggle for justice with pertinacity; but they can quickly degenerate into opiates, encouraging tranquil resignation to systemic evil and injustice.

Religious hope has down the ages generated countless movements of protest, revolution, or reform. Some of these involved the transposition into secular terms of religious language. Some were naively utopian or escapist; others engaged directly with the power structures of society. Many forms of socialism and Marxism itself have been interpreted as secular transpositions of the Judaeo-Christian hope, new ways of seeking the city that has foundations, the Kingdom of God and its justice.

The Withering of Public Hope

When Bishop Lesslie Newbigin returned to Britain after decades of ministry overseas, particularly in South India, he was often asked what was the greatest difficulty he faced in returning to Britain from India. His invariable answer was: 'The disappearance of hope.' 'Even in the most squalid slums of Madras,' he said, 'there was always the belief that things could be improved .... In spite of all the disappointments since independence came in 1947, there was still the belief in a better future ahead.' In Britain, on the other hand, the old hope, the steady confidence in a better future, appeared to have disintegrated. And this situation, Newbigin believed, poses vast problems both for western society and for Christian ministry in it.[2]

A few years later Trevor Blackwell and Jeremy Seabrook explored 'the withering of public hope'. This erosion of hope they saw as corrosive both of healthy conviviality and of a personal sense of meaning and fulfilment:

> *Rage, helplessness, a sense of redundancy; a feeling of being in exile, of disappointment and dividedness; loathing, contempt and fear, a dread of being suffocated; a disabling self-doubt.*

These are our feelings, living in Britain in the 1990s. How different they are from anything we anticipated, as we were growing up in that changed world which our parents had won for us after 1945. The future at that time seemed expansive and filled with hope, not only personal hopes, but also the belief that the society in which we were to take our place was getting better, morally as well as materially. Modest though the lives of our families might have been, we felt that they were nevertheless bequeathing to us something of great worth: a vision of a better world that was in the process of being realised. They gave us to understand that this involved a decisive break with the punishing and destructive aspects of the life they had known; and we believed them. They were even slightly envious of us, for they felt that they might not live to see the furthest consequences of the changes they had helped to enact.[3]

Newbigin, Blackwell and Seabrook remind us that hope is a central component of any life that is worth living, and a healthy society needs some kind of shared social hope. But hope is in crisis in our day. The traditional bearers of hope – utopian political movements, churches that sustain some kind of eschatological expectation, ideological systems that nourish an openness towards the future – all seem to be in decline and disarray. Is it possible in such a situation of hopelessness for hope to be reborn, for a resurrection of expectation to take place? What might this involve? And what are the responsibilities in this regard of Christians, of people who believe that the Judaeo-Christian tradition is not finally exhausted, of people who are convinced that political and social movements should nourish, explore and seek to implement a social hope which is at its heart a hope for justice?

The present situation is not without its ironies. That visionary Marxist, Ernst Bloch, wrote his vast *Das Prinzip Hoffnung*, in which he saw Marxism as the heir of the biblical emphasis on hope, at a time when Marxist regimes and most Marxists had abandoned hope as a significant theme. He was, accordingly, treated as a heretic. Then, in the 1960s, Jürgen Moltmann took up Bloch's theme, and sparked off an explosion of theological interest in the theme of hope. Once again, the owl of Minerva only takes flight when dark has fallen! For already in the 1960s a mood of disillusion was beginning. And we have to attempt to understand why this was so, why there was so rapid a disenchantment with both the broad religious and metaphysical hopes and the more specific political hopes that had sustained people for so long.

There was, first of all, a mounting sense of the bankruptcy of hopes that had failed. In the 1960s the young Alasdair MacIntyre declared that he remained a Marxist because 'the Marxist project remains the only one we have for re-establishing hope as a social virtue'.[4] A similar Marxist hope flourished in the 1930s in the poverty stricken Jewish community in the Glasgow Gorbals in which Ralph Glasser grew up, and which he depicts so powerfully in his three volume autobiography. One of their number returned with his family to the Russia they had left years before, in the belief that 'it was a new world in which the workers ruled, not the old despots who had ground the faces of the poor'. They were never heard of again.[5] Meanwhile the others met in the Gorbals to nourish their hope together:

> They sustained themselves with milkless tea and sometimes with black bread from the bakery. They talked with certainty and the passion of people who saw a bright deliverance within reach, convinced that they were in the van of those who would secure it. Listening to their throaty talk, so often punctuated by tubercular coughs and spitting, voices often raised in impatience with one another, it was possible to believe that at any moment they would compel the world to realise their dreams. Restless exiles, making a hard life in an alien environment, they nourished their souls by fixing their gaze on the far horizon, obstinately proclaiming the innocence of man and his necessary unity with all his kind. Theirs was a desperate optimism. Like storm-lost navigators they fed themselves with signs and portents.[6]

Disillusionment gradually impinged, as the awful reality of what was happening in the Stalinist utopia, the even more dreadful events in Nazi Germany, the Spanish Civil War, and mounting hardship and unemployment at home percolated into people's consciousness. The 'profound resignation' that ensued among the older generation was alarming to the young – 'Did they want us to abandon hope before we had even started?', Glasser and his contemporaries asked.[7] Similar disillusion seems to have followed every modern flourishing of hope. The trenches of the Somme put paid for many to the sunny optimism of nineteenth century liberal progressivism. The Spanish Civil War revealed for others the moral ambiguities of utopian expectations of the right and of the left. The Holocaust produced both despair and the Zionist determination to build in Palestine, the promised land, a new, secure Israel which claimed God's promises. The outburst of hope in post-war reconstruction which was embodied in the welfare state, in course of time led to the depressing conviction that it was not fulfilling adequately, and perhaps could not fulfil at all, the immense expectations which had been invested in it. Today it seems to many people that 'the winds have gone out of the sails of utopia'.

Hope, Vision, Utopia

Why are we like this? In a paradoxical way it is because we have lost hope and a vision for the world that we fear hope. The fact that we can see nothing for us makes us fear any argument that there is hope, that there might be something there. The point is that hope is a central component of any worthwhile life and that traditional bearers of hope seem to have disappeared from the stage of contemporary society. Churches with some eschatological dimension, utopian political movements, all seem in decline and in disarray. In fact one might say that the traditional bearers of hope in our society in general, and not just those at the fringe, have drawn in and have not been able to produce any new vision.

One might say that this is due to failure of intellectual effort. And this is true – but one should not see this in the abstract. For part of the problem has been the material failure of some of the hopes of the post-war era such as the problems with the welfare state and the collapse in East Europe. The more global idea of the end of, and victory in, the Cold War, which aside from the triumphalism of those such as Margaret Thatcher, has been more soberly encapsulated in theoretical form by Francis Fukuyama.[8] Here history is frozen in the triumph of liberalism or, as some might prefer to call it, the triumph of American hegemony. Francis Fukuyama proclaims that we stand at 'the end of history'. This means that there is nothing left to hope for. We have arrived. The absolute moment is now. The triumph of liberal democracy means that there is nothing further to strive for, no possibility of fundamental criticism of our consumerist society. All that is left is to fine-tune heaven. 'Liberal democracy,' writes Fukuyama, 'is the only legitimate ideology left in the world.'[9] The hopes of the past have turned sour, or shown themselves to be poisonous. We are better off without them. And so a New World Order is proclaimed, to freeze and protect the absolute moment, the end of history, at which we have arrived. What we have is not only the material failure of old hopes, but the failure intellectually to engage with this without either looking at some mythical past vision and still trying to recreate it or, in the name of realism, effectively accepting that there is nothing that can be done or thought.

We want to argue that this is something to do with the way in which hope and vision are seen. It will have been noticed that we have used, more or less interchangeably, the words hope and vision. We have done this because hope appears intimately connected with vision – the vision thing. That there is some point; that there is meaning which is, or has the potential to be, somehow (and we use the word in a non religious context) redemptive. Let us now turn then, to look at vision or, more sociologically, at utopia.

15

For Mannheim, 'a state of mind is utopian when it is incongruous with the state of reality within which it occurs'.[10] For Zygmunt Bauman[11] its original meaning has two intertwined meanings: 'place that does not exist' and 'something that is desired'. This, he says, enables one to use it, in modern times, in a pejorative and dismissive sense – 'something is merely utopian'. For we concentrate on the 'place that does not exist'. Yet of course this is strange, for as Peter Young points out,[12] the closer reality gets to the utopian vision the less likely is the thinking to be dubbed utopian. There must always be this distance – there must always be, paradoxically enough, a failure of reality to 'measure up' What this implies is that both elements are important. Looked at in this way one can see how the view that we are beginning to adumbrate differs in an important way from more usual ways of looking at utopia.

Often the metaphor used is that of a journey with some sort of ultimate destination. The idea of utopia as a blueprint, a worked-out programme, lends credence to that for it is often put as the ideal society at which we can arrive. This, from Thomas More on, has been a substantial literary genre. But we can make a distinction here and we can see it when Young talks about a problem that the idea of utopia poses for social science. For utopias seem to be neither clearly theoretical nor empirical in nature. They are, he says following Bauman, in a third category close to the idea of 'praxis' or knowledge for action. The implications of this are that utopias often appear as bad scholarship in the sense that they are slippery and elusive and arguments from utopian positions slide from one thing to another. This is because they do not denote any particular theory – it is not in fact a theory at all. Rather it is a grouping of ideas that we use not so much as a guide to our action but rather something that informs and transforms our actions.

What we mean here is that though utopias are (in a way necessarily) other- and future-directed they are not a distant beacon at the end of a road on which we travel. Their looking at the future is important in the sense that they show how intimately they are connected with hope, with optimism for the future; they need imagination and faith. But, to use the metaphor of the journey again, this is not to say that we just have to pick out a road to the hoped-for destination. It is the journey itself that is important. Our utopia, our act of hopeful imagination, is one that transforms that journey for it makes the act of travel an utopian activity in itself. We might say that part of our utopia is constructing the road that we have to travel on. And as we do this, fired by the future-directed hope, the actual destination does not have to be our paramount aim and the process of constructing the road becomes as, if not more, important. The point is that the utopian vision is something that through its future direction works in the present. In transforming our activity now, the future dwells in the present. So we might say that the significance of the eschatological thinking of the early church is that the vision of the kingdom was so strong (it was imminent) that it transformed the church's practice; it differed later when that hope was less strong. It is an active and enabling presence which transforms us and makes us the people we are here and now. In one sense the journey becomes the destination.

Now there are clearly tensions here. For one might argue that the final destination is something that cannot be denied, otherwise the hope really goes. The journey cannot take over entirely. We return to that later – at the moment we want to argue that one important thing about the vision that must not be lost sight of is that it gives sense to our activity in the here and now, it makes it hopeful and utopian. And this is not only in the sense that we see it *sub specie aeternitatis* as worthwhile because it is leading somewhere but because it is valuable in itself. If our lives were to finish we would not think them wasted because we have not arrived there; our lives are complete because of what we are doing and not because that is where we should end. Take Victor Serge. Here was a man who took part in the Russian Revolution, fought in the Spanish Civil War, was a Communist, Trotskyite, Anarchist – his life was a catalogue of failures, in the positions he took and the sides he fought on. But he never thought that his life and activities were a waste, because the hope that transformed them gave them a point – brought the future into the present and made his life complete. Which is one way perhaps, in which we can also understand the crucifixion and the resurrection – as we shall see later.

Though we have looked at and made more precise what sort of thing it is that we have lost when we talk of the lack of hope in our society, we have now to tackle a question that arises from the discussion so far. Is what we have been talking about so far merely a formal definition of the notion of hope and its connection with hope and utopia? If it is then we have a problem. For we have talked about hope and vision positively as if that is something that is good for people to have; an important thing in building our lives and our society. But many people have hopes and visions that we cannot accept; that we think are harmful. And this is not merely because we think that the vision has been used wrongly; has been in some way deformed; is highly susceptible to deformation and thus should not be entertained. Rather it is because the vision itself involves an act of imagination that is, in varying ways, false or wicked.

The distinction is implicit in the way those who wanted to counter the argument that there was no difference between communism and fascism (in its Nazi form) did so. Their argument was that communism was a deformed utopian ideology while fascism did not have this utopian transformative character. Mannheim tries to distinguish the ideological from the utopian and according to Young makes the kind of distinction that one can make between reform and revolution; reformism equals ideology and utopia equals revolution. But there is more to it than that and utopianism can change, over time, to ideology and vice versa. It all depends, says Young, on the degree of congruence with reality. The nearer it is to what is going on the more it can seem like reformism. For what defines the utopian mentality must have some degree of transcendence. At the same time since, as we saw, this form of thinking puts the future in the present, it must have its roots in 'reality', in the here and now. The danger then is that the more the vision is 'realistic', the more it will be involved in short-term political aims and solutions, losing sight of that transcendence which is necessary to the utopian vision. And yet it is in that space between the transcendent and the real that we must operate. That is where we must be.

The 'Realsozialismus' of Central and Eastern Europe was clearly unrealistic and we cannot go back to that, or anything like it now. Transcendence must have some roots in reality otherwise it cannot be said to be transcendent. But at the same time it must stand outside that reality and transform our actions within and thus transform it. The key notions then are transcendence and transformation and it is through those that we can begin to filter out false hopes. For central to the notion of hope, we will argue, is the idea of a transformative vision; one that makes our lives and activities complete because paradoxically, as we shall argue later, they are unfinished and there can be no finish for them.

Loss of Hope and Vision

The best way of understanding the above point is to look to what is involved, at the level of society, in the loss of hope. There are two ways in which it might be said that we lose hope. First we can lose hope because there is nothing left to hope for. For those who are totally politically and socially disadvantaged there is no hope left. John Kenneth Galbraith[13] makes this case. He points to a group in the capitalist societies of the fortunate and contented. This, in these societies, is now no longer a few but rather a majority, at least a majority of those who take part in the political process. How can we characterise this 'culture of contentment'? (a) They think that they have their just deserts. What they want and have is achieved by their worth. (b) They are enamoured of 'short termism' – they will always prefer short-term solutions to long-run ones because the future might not arrive and thus they would have lost out to it. (c) They want to keep the state 'off people's backs', especially if this means paying higher taxes. (d) There is the toleration of great disparities in income. The toleration of the very rich is accepted because not to do so would threaten their own income as against the very poor. In short they are happy in the position that they are in and all their work goes to preserve it.

Second, against this, Galbraith posits the 'underclass' which has always been found necessary in capitalist societies to do the work that the fortunate found disagreeable but was necessary to keep them in their affluence. In the past mobility (and the possibility of mobility) from that class to the favoured class prevented eruptions of discontent on a large scale. The class was fluid and always needed to be replenished with new members. But now, he says, things have changed and transition becomes more difficult. The group becomes structurally fixed, structural unemployment comes in and more and more social groups are threatened with being sucked back into it. This makes the possibility of containment harder and harder and explosions more likely.

What Galbraith is saying is that, more and more in these societies is to be found a group of people who have no hope because there is no possibility for them of getting anywhere; and that there are a lot of people, the 'contented', who do not want to go anywhere. Though this is based on the American experience, one can see parallels in Scotland and Britain. There is no hope for the former because there seem absolutely no possibilities of action. They opt out of the political process which increasingly becomes one that is only used by the contented and which is concerned mainly with protecting the structure of contentment with small shifts allowed in. In one way the world of the former seems hopeless and the lack of hope is manifested in sporadic violence and riots from which the contented guard themselves in what increasingly become fortress settlements of the contented. And of course this is not action that is informed by hope, but rather the bitterness of desolation which leads to destruction rather than transformation. However, one might say, there is little possibility of self-delusion for one can see the hopelessness head on. It is clear, at any rate, that one needs a vision and a hope. It was not by chance that Dante emblazoned the gates of Hell with the slogan 'Abandon Hope All Ye Who Enter Here'.

But what we are interested in here is also the nature of the contentment of the fortunate. For they also have no hope. For them, hope has become redundant and any kind of utopianism is dismissed out of hand. They are happy to believe that this is the best of all possible worlds because, for them, it is. They have arrived where they were wanting to go, the 'End of History has come' and the 'New World has arrived', so there is no need for hope and vision.

But there is another way of looking at this. It is not that there is no need for hope, rather what we have is a state of hopelessness. For they are not so much contented with what they have as frightened of losing it. Their policies, as shown by Galbraith, are motivated by the fear of loss. They have what they want and want nothing new, but perhaps more of the same. They have no transformative vision; their only vision, and their only hope, is of a world that might be like the present one, but bigger. They are like the servant who, in the parable, buried his talent in the earth. That parable should not be seen as a Thatcherite parable, but rather one about hope and vision and fear. The way to lose your life is to protect it and defend it and do nothing more. If you have no hope and no vision then you will act as the servant who, full of fear of the master, buried the talent entrusted to him in the ground so as to protect it. In trying to defend what you have, you will, as did the servant, lose even that. The point is that you need hope and vision in order to be able to see and risk the possibilities in your life. What the parable is saying is that to be content in the way Galbraith has been describing is to be in a kind of fear; to be truly hopeless because you can see no possibility beyond that which you have. And in that that becomes all you want, the possibility of transformation becomes dangerous and threatening. And one can see this the more as the world becomes increasingly unstable and that instability threatens the fortunate. This form of contentment closes individuals off both from themselves and from the world – they do not want the world to be anything other than it is; they want it to be flat and hopeless. In this sort of world change, and the vision and hope that inspire it, are dangerous – better the devil [sic] that you know.

It might seem as though here we are looking at the problems from the point of view of the fortunate and not addressing those for whom there is nothing at all – not even that false contentment which is, one might say, better than nothing at all. But if this is so it is only again because of the realities of the matter. The contented have the power. The Conservatives win general election after general election because the majority of people are in work and their standard of living is still acceptable – 'you've never had it so good' works for them. But the parable tells us that they are destroying their lives and they do not know it. People vote for tax cuts rather than social welfare. They cannot see that they need vision to save their lives and so they block change and transformation. Those in our first category, who have nothing, they at least see this clearly.

Notes to Chapter 1

1. *The Kingdom of God and History* (1938 Oxford Conference Series), pp 56-7.
2. Lesslie Newbigin: *The Other Side of 1984: Questions for the Churches* (London: British Council of Churches, 1983), pp 3-4.
3. Trevor Blackwell and Jeremy Seabrook: *The Politics of Hope: Britain at the End of the Twentieth Century* (London: Faber, 1988), pp 3-4.
4. Alasdair MacIntyre: *Marxism and Christianity* (Harmondsworth: Penguin, 1968), p 88. Much of MacIntyre's complex intellectual pilgrimage and return to Christian faith might be interpreted as the search for a sure grounding for hope. This book is a rewriting of *Marxism – An Interpretation* (London: SCM Press, 1953), which MacIntyre wrote when he was still a Christian. In that book he said: 'If the Christian hope is to be realised in history, it must assume the form of a political hope; it must use the morally ambiguous means which are the only means to attain political ends. In other words, the religious content must be realised in political terms. But this is exactly what the young Marx did in his criticism of religion. Marxism is in essence a complete realisation of Christian eschatology' (p 120).
5. Ralph Glasser: *Growing up in the Gorbals* (London: Pan, 1987), p 6.
6. Glasser (op. cit.), p 7.
7. Glasser (op. cit.), p 47.
8. Francis Fukuyama: *The End of History and the Last Man* (New York: Avon Books, 1992).
9. Francis Fukuyama in *The Guardian*, 17 September 1990.
10. K. Mannheim: *Ideology and Utopia: An Introduction to the Sociology of Knowledge* (London: Routledge Kegan Paul, 1936).
11. Z. Bauman: *Socialism: The Active Utopia* (London: Allen and Unwin, 1976).
12. P. Young: 'The Importance of Utopias in Criminological Thinking' in *British Journal of Criminology,* 32 (1992), p 423-237.
13. J. K. Galbraith: *The Culture of Contentment* (London: Sinclair-Stevenson, 1992).

CHAPTER 2

From Hope
to Structured Generosity

Religious Hope

IS it surprising that Charles Davis can declare that 'religious hope is an area of human experience and history riddled with deception', and call for 'a therapeutic critique to purify religious hope from neurotic and ideological elements'? Religious hope, he continues, has been used as a compensation to legitimate social oppression and injustice, and as a way of avoiding facing the negativities of life and even the reality of death itself. We need therefore to struggle to find an authentic Christian hope, which in some sense is strongly validated from within the tradition, which itself has a tension between an other-worldly and a this-worldly interpretation of hope.[1]

It is universally acknowledged that the early church had close to the heart of its faith an eschatological expectation that the end was at hand, that the time of judgement was now, that a new and very different order was about to break in. This eschatology was expressed not in individualistic terms but by way of the great social and systemic images of the city, the new Jerusalem, and above all, of the Kingdom or Reign of God. The gospel was proclaimed as the good news of the Kingdom, which is not something we build, but a reality which will be graciously given to us by God. Meanwhile, the faithful are to seek the Kingdom and its justice, prefiguring that Kingdom and that justice in their common life, and judging the kingdoms of this world by the glimpses they have been given of the coming Kingdom and its characteristics. In the *Letter to the Hebrews* the life of faith is presented as a constant, lifelong seeking of the city whose builder and maker is God. Here it is faith that gives substance to hope and faith that sustains hope. 'Faith gives substance to our hopes and convinces us of realities we do not see.'[2]

Yet biblical scholars almost universally agree that even within the New Testament period, as the church became more confident, prosperous and established, the urgency of the expectation, the hope that the present order would be replaced waned. And down the centuries, eschatology and hope have tended to decline in mainstream Christianity, and to be left to survive in millenarian sects and movements on the margins, whenever the church has become overly confident, secure, prosperous, powerful and respected. In the nineteenth century, for example, the Last Things became little more than an appendix in dogmatics textbooks rather than a living and central dimension of faith. The liberal belief in progress was something quite different from the Christian hope. It saw the building of the heavenly city as a cumulative human project, which was already well underway. If one had not already arrived at Jerusalem, at least the foundations had been well and truly laid. The optimism about progress showed itself incapable of developing any serious critique of things as they are, because they are regarded as the necessary foundations of the future. Liberal theology served to endorse this sunny view of progress. Albert Schweitzer, in the afterglow of nineteenth century liberalism, portrayed Jesus as a 'stranger' who was inaccessible to us precisely because he came from a context of eschatology, apocalyptic, hope which is totally different from ours.

Then came the First World War, the rise of Hitler, and the Holocaust. With this, liberal theology appeared to collapse for a time at least, and theologians like Barth and Bultmann in their differing ways rediscovered eschatology and apocalyptic. It was as if themes and images which had lain more or less dormant for centuries suddenly sprang to life. People found that eschatology, and even the more lurid imagery of apocalyptic, were necessary if they were to understand what was going on around them; and hope was essential if they were to act faithfully, justly and wisely in a world that was full of evil and oppression. This is the process that Austin Farrer referred to as 'the rebirth of images' – ideas that most people thought were dead and buried, but still survive, submerged beneath the surface as it were, in the canon and in the tradition, particularly at the margins, spring suddenly into life.

Sociologists like Norman Cohn and Vittorio Lanternari have famously argued that marginal sects and groupings of the oppressed have nurtured millenarian, apocalyptic and messianic forms of faith, most markedly in a Judaeo-Christian context. The early church was clearly such a community, reaching forward in hope to an alternative reality, an open future, God's gift rather than a human achievement. Bloch and Cohn in particular have shown how Judaeo-Christian eschatology not only provided themes and resources for messianic and apocalyptic sects (which were frequently persecuted by the official church), but also flowed into modern secular social and political movements of protest, reform and revolution.

But is it possible any longer for religious images to be reborn, for a religious account of hope to become once more influential? Can the Christian faith any longer sustain a living and relevant hope in cold times? The German philosopher Peter Sloterdijk doubts it. Both classical metaphysics and Christian theology, he argues, have outlived their public relevance: 'Both have undergone a historical process resembling mummification. Religion and fundamental philosophy have continued an existence in which they have outlived their usefulness over against the world and reality. They are scholastic ghost towns, uninhabitable and no longer plausible'.[3] He has a point. But is it possible that the image of a relevant and challenging hope can be reborn with the gospel as midwife? Can the expectancy which lies at the heart of the gospel, the refusal to regard the present as absolute, final, the belief in an open future and the confidence that grace will be given us in the future be purified and rekindled in the public realm? Can Christian faith regenerate the hope for justice? Can people again believe in promise? Is it possible in this age to spell out the relation between the hope of the Kingdom of God and the search for justice and peace in this world? Can the winds of utopia blow again in our age?

These must remain open questions. But there is also some evidence which suggests that religion is not in fact as 'mummified' as many people in the West believe. Even in cold times – perhaps especially when the atmosphere is icy – faith may still have the capacity to sustain and shape a social hope with clear political relevance. For St Paul, hope is like the pains of childbirth. The new is coming into being, and we await it with eager expectancy:

> Up to the present, as we know, the whole created universe in all its parts groans as if in the pangs of childbirth. What is more, we also, to whom the Spirit is given as the firstfruits of the harvest to come, are groaning inwardly while we look forward eagerly to our adoption, our liberation from mortality. It was with this hope that we were saved. Now to see something is no longer to hope: why hope for what is already seen? But if we hope for something we do not yet see, then we look forward to it eagerly and with patience.[4]

This patient waiting is not at all acquiescence or resignation, but an active and confident seeking of the fulfilment of God's promises.

It is the attitude that sustained Bonhoeffer both in his resistance to Hitler, and in his martyrdom. He wrote just before his arrest:

> *There are people who regard it as frivolous, as some Christians think it impious, for anyone to hope and prepare for a better earthly future. They think that the meaning of present events is chaos, disorder, and catastrophe; and in resignation or pious escapism they surrender all responsibility for reconstruction and for future generations. It may be that the day of judgement will dawn tomorrow; in that case, we shall gladly stop working for a better future, but not before.*[5]

This kind of hope keeps people going when all around seems hopeless. In the South African theologian Denise Ackermann's words, 'it acts like a powerful alchemy enabling human beings to emerge from ghastly circumstances with their humanity intact .... Hope is resistance. It actively resists the void of hopelessness'.[6]

Realism and Vision

We have see then, how the parable of the talents shows us how hope and vision are necessary for our lives – for otherwise we lose them. Thus one way that we can distinguish true hope from that that which passes for hope is by its transformative character. At the same time however we saw that the vision must be grounded in realism, must engage with the situation as we find it. We must not completely discount the fears of loss and predictability. But we must not let it close our minds to those who have nothing at all. Galbraith said it was characteristic of the culture of contentment that it would do nothing and would thus produce no vision for transformation. The politics of contentment are pretty powerful.

We might say however that things, in Britain at least, are changing in that a vision that is both transcendent and realistic is being offered. And so we go back to Iain MacWhirter and see the new vision of a politics infused with Christian hope. Though MacWhirter attacks the linking of Christianity and politics, it is clear that, in a general way, as against the self-referentiality that went on before, some sort of vision seems to be entering politics. Though this is oppositional, it cannot be conceived in party-political terms and is thus not so much a look at New Labour as an attempt to understand the sort of vision that the broad grouping of which that is a part represents. Are politics beginning really to talk of values and vision? Were our earlier comments about the absence of values from the discourse of Parliamentary politics wrong and MacWhirter is merely arguing against the too close association of religion and politics conceived in relatively narrow terms? The vision that we are thinking of is one that is trying to preserve what is seen as good in the market and the market solutions while at the same time trying to show that this need not preclude welfare orientation and a commitment to transform the lives of the wretched in our societies without relying on some notion of the 'trickle-down' effect: an effect which Galbraith famously describes a hoping that 'if one feeds the horse enough oats, some will pass through to the road for the sparrows'.[7] The vision includes a commitment to social justice, but one which argues that social justice is something that cannot be divorced from efficiency. Indeed social justice is necessary for economic efficiency. It is indeed a great thing when moral interest combines with self interest – but the history of these claims – 'what is good for General Motors is good for the country' – behoves us to treat them with at least caution. Does this general raft of policies achieve this? Does it give us a realistic vision?

We want to approach this not by looking at the detail of that vision as such, or even particular instances of it. Rather we want to look at the nature of the vision and thus the hope that it calls on. We want to start with Duncan Forrester[8] who, in a comment on the report of The Commission on Social Justice chaired by Gordon Borrie, looks at the nature of vision. Historically vision was something that always came from the margins, something that small groups nurtured and then tried to get people to coalesce around. The image is one of a snowball which when rolled along a field of snow gradually grows bigger. His examples are the vision that fuelled the post-war welfare state and the Thatcherite vision. But he sees something different in the report of the Borrie Commission. For there, as Borrie says, the commission tried to get at what people would all readily agree to and that this is one of its main strengths.

We are confident that at least in our belief that there is such a thing as 'social justice', we reflect the common sense of the vast majority of ordinary people …. What the various arguments about entitlement and desert suggest seems to be close to what many people believe: that there is basic justice in people having some differential reward for their productive activities. It is not simply self interest, or again scepticism about government spending programmes … that makes people resist the idea that everyone's income is in principle a resource for redistribution; that idea

26

also goes against their sense of what is right … we have attempted to articulate some widely-held feelings about the character of our society.[9]

Part of the point of a vision is to provide the scope for transforming our lives and our activities by bring the future into the present. It shapes and transforms the things we do so that they have point and meaning, so that they can be understood in the context of a more just and loving society. But since it shapes and transforms, it cannot wholly come from what people now think, from present day consensus, that would precisely, as we saw above, make it non utopian and non visionary. Forrester links this with the Rawlsian methodology[10] of reflective equilibrium. The notion that one takes the 'considered convictions' of people in a society, refines and re-orders them and then re-tests them against the convictions again, continuing this dialectical process until some sort of reflective equilibrium is found. We do not want to deny that this is a powerful tool for moral philosophy, but the problem with it is that it can easily fall foul of the argument that what you get out is merely what you believe in the first place. In the case of Rawls it is that the society considered behind the 'veil of ignorance' is not surprisingly one that reflects the views of American East Coast liberals. In the context of the Commission on Social Justice, the fear is that reflection of what people actually think, instead of providing some transcendental vision that points to activities that are just and loving will reflect precisely those politics and views of people that it wanted to get away from. Thus it becomes something that is about winning an election – providing policies that will get votes rather than providing a vision for the people. The problem with reflective equilibrium is that in this context it can become remarkably like vote catching and politics becomes, as was argued above, a self-referential system concerned with getting votes. One might say then that the steady deterioration in recent years in this country has led to a loss of real hope and its substitution by the false hope that is no hope but only the achievement of more of the same or the same for more.

The Mirror of Hope

Thus a vision can become just an expression of the contented and of their lack of hope or fear of hope; reflective equilibrium can merely reflect back our society to us. What we see is our group or ourselves reflected back. We might think that there is a grand vision but what we are reflecting back is our own and our group's contentment. Our realism in the face of the other is ourselves reflected back. In a complex modern world, what happens is that there is more and more splitting off into separate systems, like the law, economics, politics which are functionally differentiated. What this means is that these systems operate with their own logic and codes into which information from other systems cannot enter without being translated into the receiving system's code. In effect the system cannot understand anything outside itself except in its own terms. For example, law and economics are systems in the sense that we have been talking about. To a business person a parking offence and the fine that is paid might be an overhead in the business that they run, while to the law it is a crime. To the criminologist the question raised by more severe sentencing policies are those of deterrence and justice while to the politician they raise questions of votes. What this means is that these systems cannot look outside of themselves, for they recognise no outside that is not translated in the system's own terms and, since that is the case, it is as though there is no outside. They appear to look outside but they are merely reflecting themselves back in. Individuals can also be seen as systems like this. When they look out all they see is, like Narcissus, themselves. And this is the moral message that these sort of theories send and why they cannot produce vision. When, in this mode, we try and reach out all we see is ourselves in the mirror that we have created. Our incommensurable discourses do not adjust to others, they adjust to themselves. All they see is themselves in the mirror that they have created. They think that they are doing things for others but in reality they are doing things for themselves. The world breaks down into self absorbed circles, secure and confident in their righteousness. We delude ourselves that we care for others when we only care for ourselves. We leave smoke filled rooms thinking we have done something and all we have done is increase our wealth and power. Everything is lost in the reflection of self. Think of America's 'New World Order' and the new order in Europe. We have become trapped in our discourses. Worse, unlike Kafka, we like it. We do not see anything beyond but we don't care.

Politicians and others trapped in the system in this way, while thinking they are seeking to help others, are simply seeking their own power or transferring their own wants onto others, other being only mirrors of themselves and not the other. Let us look at this with respect to East/Central Europe and the Thatcherite vision. There one might say that the Thatcherite vision, or something like it, holds sway. And one can see, in many institutions in those societies, the emancipation and freedom which that vision gave or was seen as giving. Some people reacted positively to it and thought it would help transform people's lives in those societies. But to some extent what they saw was the rest of the societies in their image. It had emancipated them personally and therefore everyone else was assumed to be emancipated. They did not notice those who could not get into the market, who were left behind by the marketisation of these societies. They only saw those in the market and their prosperity. They only saw its greed. What that group did was create people in its own image and thus there was no possibility of transformation of themselves – in fact that is what is guarded against. Efficiency, prosperity and social justice, say the Borrie Commission, go hand in hand, or as Margaret Thatcher famously said – the Good Samaritan was only able to do so because he was rich. The transformative possibilities that this might not be the case and that, in reaching out and giving, we might radically change ourselves and the world are ignored. And so there is no hope – only the hope and vision to guard what you have and in the process of guarding that you lose it.

Think of the discussion about 'workfare' and the part that this might play in the new vision. In a way again it is the contented seeing the world in their own image. Everyone is, or is potentially able to be, autonomous and self regarding – master or mistress of all they survey. We are told, in clear echoes of the Thatcherite slogan of the 'dependency culture' that 'dependency' is bad. Social security must to some extent be worked for so that people are not dependent to their detriment. We must do this so that they can be like us. If they do not succeed then it is through their own inaction and through their own dismerit. The fear is of a vision which might mean the image of autonomous free-ranging person is shattered. That we, who see ourselves as independent and autonomous, might be dependent as well. And we fear the transformative possibilities of that risking of ourselves with others and in others. That is something that, like the servant in the parable of the talents, we fear.

Love and Hope

We have argued so far that vision must be realistic or else it cannot make sense. Since if we do not start from the now we lose
touch with what it is we wish to transform. Then the future does
not come into and transform the present since it is in a faraway
place which only has locus in that future. And the consequences
of that are we cultivate a 'beautiful soul' and forget about the
wicked world. And, of course, this is what MacWhirter says Christianity should be when he claims that it is too pure to get into the
'dirty business of politics'. Many believe and act as if this should
be so and we saw above how that is to do with contentment and
the fear of any hope that might shatter that contentment. But
there is a double fear here. First there is the fear that we might lose
what we have – the affluent will vote to keep themselves affluent
and will not vote for tax cuts, for example. Second there is – and
this is clearly implied in MacWhirter – a fear of what might loose-
ly be called 'contamination'. We fear the 'dirty business of politics'
because we do not want to lose our purity, we might be as contaminated as they are.

It is both these anxieties that prevent us from acting in what
Gillian Rose calls the 'middle'.[11] The first fear in the guise of
rationality, that 'social justice, wealth and efficiency are inextricably connected', breaks down into the particularity of selfishness
and greed. The second fear doesn't want to venture into the pit
because it fears that what it does might be wrong. It is fearful of
entering a world where there is no certainty; where the possibility
of transformation means the possibility of upsetting the certainty
and the contentment that has been built up. As soon as there is the
possibility of change there is the possibility of error and that is
what we also fear. So, we try to devise systems that do not fail or
rather which do not enable us to contemplate the possibility of
error. And so the two anxieties roll into one. The autonomy which
we project on to others because we hate to be dependent ourselves, and fear the transformative power and risk of that dependence, becomes safe as it is reflected back to us as the rational system
of our greed which is always right. And so ironically we do
become dependent; slaves to our own greed. Macwhirter's point
then is something that points to the consequences of the lack of
hope in general – its seemingly humble 'you are too good for us'
hides the way we all shun vision and thus become slaves to ourselves. Everything becomes a mirror to our wants and our greed.

Unless we break the mirror and see the objects of our policy as they are rather than as reflections of ourselves, we do not treat them as anything other than our instruments – we make what we want of you, we are tyrants. How do we break through that mirror? Why should we do otherwise? To do so requires a risk – it entails the risk of not only failing but also of being wrong, of being contaminated. So we need the hope and vision to take that risk because otherwise we are condemned to the comfort zone which is the ultimate corruption.

What offers us vision to do otherwise? Consider God – all powerful and all loving. He creates us in His own image. But we are not just His creatures. He allows us autonomy, risks the introduction of caprice and will into His comfortable system world. Why? Because of His love. We can develop this parable of creation on into the Cross. God, in creating autonomous beings who are not merely in his image but reflect themselves as well as Him, puts Himself at their mercy, laying Himself open to what they may do to Him. This *kenosis* or self-emptying is seen in the crucifixion, the terrifying giving of self which is the giving away of everything with no knowledge or guarantee of what will ensue. God empties Himself into the world and thus puts Himself at the mercy of His creation. Resurrection is neither foreseen nor a reversal of that giving away. In this act God takes on both the anxieties that we have talked about for a vision, the possibility/hope of the transformation of the world. He risks annihilation, for the Tomb is only unlocked when we recognise and enter into that crucifixion; it is only then that God lives in the world. It is then that one can say that the concrete instantiation of the Divine is in the Other.

Then shall the king say to them that shall be on his right hand: come ye blessed of my Father, possess you the kingdom prepared for you from the foundation of the world. For I was hungry, and you gave me to eat; I was thirsty and you gave me to drink; I was a stranger and you took me in.

(St Matthew 25: 34-35)

The significance of this epigram is not that God watches over everyone and to hurt one of the poor is to hurt God – a sort of cosmic non-aggression pact. Rather it is that God is in them. And this has a double significance because it also shows how God takes the risk of being like His creation. Not merely as in the poor, but in the corrupt and wrong. He risks His resurrection being made

31

corrupt – and Churches, in their actions over the ages, have shown that to be well founded.

This appears to us to be one of the central images of Christianity. The crucifixion is the key moment of the resurrection. God dies on the cross and lives again in the world; vulnerable to His creation. The transfigured body of Christ is in the world but His existence depends on us. If we reject Him by refusing to build the law of love in the world then He will indeed be dead. That was the risk He takes out of love – we can take no other. But one must not understand this *via crucis* as a grand romantic gesture, throwing away all reason in a dramatic gesture of love. It is not an ethic of sacrifice, for the Borrie Commission is right if we think of good in the Aristotelian sense of *eudaimonia* (faring well) and not purely in an economic context. Rather it is an act of rational love for both are inextricably implicated. We cannot just swap our desires for someone else's. We need to create a society where we view all interests from a non positional point of view. But this process of negotiation means a loss to ourselves so that we can find ourselves in the transformation. And we need the love to be able to make that jump from the security of our fastnesses to the risk of transformation. To do that we need vision; the love only works if we do have some vision of what we are about and so reason is implicated in the jump as well. This then is the vision that is necessary for social justice for it enables our love to act and give ourselves up to the poor here and the Third World because that is the process of the transformation of ourselves and the world.

But what is important too is to recognise that the jump is the acting-out of the vision. It is not for the dream of some future state that we act as we do, but in our hope-inspired act we act in the future now – we bring the future into the present. And that helps us to deal with the most terrifying possibility of all, of error, of failure and corruption. We take the risk because, to use the metaphor of the journey again, the destination becomes the journey and it is the risky passage that is the future now. The only way that we can save our lives is by losing them to this uncharted and risky journey otherwise we truly lose them. But we must finally emphasise that this is not an irrational journey, we are not trying to claim that all you need is love or good intentions for the vision sustaining that loving jump must have sense and reason. That is why the epigram from Matthew above is so apposite. For in recognising the divine in the sick, the poor and the wicked, we see the reason in our act of love. For the rational, loving community is there in that person. We see together the possibilities of failure, reason and love. For Christians too that is the mystery which we encounter in the Eucharist and which gives us the strength to go forward. It is in that sense too that the vision must be 'realistic' and the new realism of the radical parties is not to be discarded; one must also not fall prey to the fear of being 'reformist' or not radical enough.

Much of what we have been saying is, as can readily be seen, about the conditions of action in the world. How the condition of our acting with reason demands an act of faith in reason at least. And that act of faith brings in the possibility of error and failure and it is there that risk and love begin. For it is that which gives us the strength not to concentrate on building a society where our thought is merely to guard against failure but to risk the genuine transformation that accepting the possibility of error brings. For that enables us to have a society where, in renegotiating with others our wants and our interests, we can gain ourselves by losing ourselves. We deal with the way in which we might now think of this society of 'structured generosity' in more practical terms in the following chapters.

Notes to Chapter 2

1. Charles Davis: *Religion and the Making of Society* (Cambridge: Cambridge University Press, 1994), pp 199–200.
2. Hebrews 11: 1.
3. Cited in a typescript by Jan Greven: 'The Failure of Utopian Expectations', 1990.
4. Romans 8: 22–25.
5. Dietrich Bonhoeffer: *Letters and Papers from Prison* (London: SCM Press, 1971), pp 15–16.
6. Denise Ackermann: 'The Alchemy of Hope' in *A Book of Hope,* pp 28–29.
7. (op. cit.), p 29.
8. Duncan B. Forrester: 'What is Social Justice?' in Andrew Morton (ed): *Justice and Prosperity: A Realistic Vision* (Edinburgh: Centre for Theology and Public Issues, New College, The University of Edinburgh, 1995).
9. *Social Justice, Strategies for National Renewal* (London: Vintage, 1994), pp 4,13,19.
10. J. Rawls: *A Theory of Justice* (Oxford: Oxford University Press, 1971).
11. G. Rose: *The Broken Middle* (Oxford: Blackwell, 1992).

CHAPTER 3

Hope in Post-War Britain

IN Chapter 1 we suggested that transformative hope is essential to personal and social good and, in Chapter 2, that hope has to act in 'the middle' ground of uncertainty if it is to establish a society characterised by 'structured generosity'. In order to explore the hope of 'structured generosity', we first turn to an analysis of the two major visions of Britain in the past fifty years: the post-war welfare state settlement and its displacement, if not replacement, by Thatcherism. We turn to this post-war experience in detail in order to take stock of our current context before turning, in Part Three, to the nature of possible contemporary hope. In particular we will re-assess the nature of the post-war settlement arguing that it contained many socialised, if not socialist, practices which have been ignored or under-valued by recent commentators and critics; we will examine in more detail the nature of the Thatcherite critique of this welfare state settlement and the alternative vision offered; we will seek to establish what the grounds are on which a new form of hope might be established. We will address this history through three questions.

First we have argued previously both that hope is essential to a healthy personal and social life and that this hope has neither to be a celebration of the present (albeit bigger) nor an unattainable other land safely removed from having to engage with current, messy, realities. Raymond Williams recounts how, sat at home on the edge of the Fens, he read a book about the recent death of old society of rural England passed down from time immemorial.[1] This, for Williams triggered the recollection of a long line of authors, from Sturt and Hardy at the turn of the twentieth century back to Hesiod in the ninth century BC, all of whom mourned the ever-recent death of the Golden Age of stable, organic, traditional society, safely back just over the past horizon. This ideology of the Golden Age functions to offer a pseudo critique of contemporary society necessarily ineffective through its reliance on a nostalgic reconstruction of, and longing for, an imagined past of harmony and plenty. The 'middle' cannot be contemplated and real social relations cannot be changed. If hope is to be more than such a nostalgia in the future tense then we must explore how hope can be both rooted in the present but point to a different future; how it can guide a journey without pre-defining its destination. *Is hope an ever-enticing state safely just over the next horizon?*

Second, to date in discussing hope we have implicitly been using two couplets: the collective and the personal; the moral and the material. The temptation when using such terms is to link the personal with the moral, the collective with the material. Such a tendency plays straight into the hands of Galbraith's culture of contentment where morality becomes solely a matter of individual conscience and the collectivity becomes a matter of what the tax-payer can afford. In exploring the problem of 'structured generosity' we need to try to think the personal and the collective in combination with the moral and the material. The two hopes of the post-war era can be seen as very different combinations of these four terms. *How can we think of hope as both personal **and** collective, material **and** moral?*

Third, we have used a distinction between authentic and false hopes. Such a distinction is necessary if we are not fall into a relativism where we must tolerate intolerance to the point of Nazism. While such a distinction may be grounded in personal Christian values this does not establish it for societies where Christian values may be given very different interpretations by different groups or may be the beliefs of a minority. *How can we differentiate between authentic and false hopes on generalizable grounds?*

The Post-War Settlement

By the post-war settlement we mean the over-arching consensus which existed for some thirty years following the 1939-45 war about the role of the state in providing 'welfare' services as part of a social wage. Treating this era as a unity for our current purposes is not to deny the real conflicts, differences and changes which occurred, but to address the high level consensus which did exist around the formation and continuation of the welfare state. The roots of this settlement lay in the traumas of the previous twenty years: the deep economic crisis of the depression and its differential effects on social classes; the experience of total war against a genocidal regime. These experiences, encapsulated in 'war radicalism', highlighted not only the inequalities of British society but, crucially, the incompetence of the upper class (Colonel Blimp *et al*) and its more than casual flirtation with Nazism. The experience of victory was the experience of the causal power of the ordinary people in all aspects of the 'war effort'. Where 'Homes Fit For Heroes' had seemed an adequate response to the 1914-18 war, something more encompassing was needed in 1945.

The post-war settlement may, in part, be characterised by Beveridge's five Giants blocking the road to social reconstruction: Want, Disease, Squalor, Ignorance and Idleness. This potent image organises many themes: current social malaise, in this case, the disruption of war and the loss of hegemony of the old order, is assumed; a case for a new form of society is also assumed (the road ...); the fairy tale opposition of good and evil (in the form of the Giants) is harnessed to this mission; the precise nature of the evils is defined.

The achievements of this settlement in the two decades after the war in facing, if not defeating, the Giants, need little documentation: a Social Security system to prevent (absolute) poverty; a National Health Service free(ish) at the point of need; a myriad of housing and planning initiatives to replace slums with 'modern' housing; an education system which met the demand for free secondary education for all; a state increasingly willing to intervene to maintain employment. While none of these initiatives were unproblematic, and indeed provided much fertile ground for the Thatcherite critique, they represented a substantial socialised sector at the heart of British society. Less noticed by recent commentators was the substantial and growing economic forms which developed, at a minimum, outwith classical capitalist relations or, at a maximum, embryonic, new economic relations in a 'mixed' economy: the public corporations running the utilities (*eg* the Post Office, British Rail); the industries nationalised as the 'commanding heights' (*eg* coal and steel); the industries bought out by the state to protect employment or strategically important industrial sectors (*eg* British Leyland, Rolls Royce); the mutual finance organisations (*eg* Building Societies and some insurance companies); the trust-based pension funds of many state sectors and of some private sectors.

Because of the particular role played by nationalised industries in the post-war UK economy, it is important to offer a somewhat terse account of some of the key elements in that experience. The form of the 'public corporation', with its conventional reliance on management expertise, emerged out of debates and argument inside the Labour movement led by advocates of a strong element of workers' representation and control. It was ironic that the re-organisation of West Germany's heavy industries immediately after the war offered a more direct and influential role for workers' elected representatives in managerial direction, a sharing of responsibilities, and that this was put through in co-operation with the then British Control Commission at a time when the much stronger UK trade unions were being told they were not yet 'ready' for such a role, and were offered no more than consultation rights of a formal kind.

In a number of cases, public corporations (and the health service) in fact took over local government plants and property which had been built up over many years of 'municipal socialism'; it was not all (fully compensated) transfer from the private sector. A major pressure for such centralised re-organisation was a recog-nition of the need for a planned co-ordination and renovation of an entire 'utility' sector, in place of inadequate and piecemeal earlier development. The key industry that most needed this was the one that 'got away' – steel. Had the early post-war national-isation been maintained (instead of being largely unwound by the incoming Conservative administration) a re-organisation on the basis of modern integrated steel plants would have gone through in the 1950s, as it actually did in South Wales. Instead the dynastic structure of steel company ownership delayed major reorganisation, under a second attempt at public ownership, until late into the 1960s – disastrously too late.

In general the chosen role for the public corporations meant a heavy use of (borrowed) capital for investment that massively reduced employment in the industries that had earlier been high-ly labour intensive (coal, railways, steel, the utilities). There was no coherent debate about the fact that the publicly-owned sector of productive industry shed employment on a large scale and over a protracted period; little attempt was made to re-think functions, or accept in practice responsibility for job creation; diversification was for much of the time politically blocked. Even the 1945 Labour Government had built in guarantees to private industry against diversification, denounced as 'creeping' socialism, in its legislation carrying through public ownership.

Over much of the period the policies actually pursued meant that the nationalised industries were exploited by capitalist industry; supply contracts for capital equipment were monopolised by United Kingdom firms, often technically backward and cartelised. Increasingly, the handling of prices, finance, borrowing terms, capital expenditure came under Treasury control, and was used within short-run concerns about inflation, demand management, etc. The routinisation of much of the function of these industries, since innovation, joint-ventures, and so on, were substantially repressed, did not help managerial creativity. Internal structures were modelled on the large private sector monopolistic firms, with multi-level hierarchies. Not only was much of this modelled on ICI, there was a moment in the 1950s when the then head of ICI was called in to review Coal Board management and recommended yet another tier of management to add to the four that already existed.

A rethinking of function to extend actual services or development activities to meet social needs was all too limited. Some aspects of this were sustained in railways and their finance (but within a starved investment programme). A good example of attempts to meet social need was the earlier post-war emphasis on rural electrification. Formal structures of accountability contrasted with the blurred relations of power and intervention between government ministers, departments and, of course, the Treasury, and the public corporation. Government did not take kindly to open accountability and public scrutiny and when an effective House of Commons committee emerged for a while it was subsequently rendered ineffective.

All this suggests that there is substantially more to the objective of socialising industries and services than the formal process of transfer of ownership. The opportunities for effective employee participation, for public accountability and for careful discussion of social and economic objectives were neglected. The organisational forms adopted also needed to be subject to revision and experimentation; the centralised control of massive re-organisation might perhaps have been followed by more diversity and de-centralisation (eg perhaps electricity and gas should have been directly linked, within a Scottish region). There could, above all, have been more commitment to the idea that a continuing effort was needed to honour the objective of 'the best obtainable system of popular administration and control'.

Addressing our first question – whether hope is always about what is always just over the next horizon – we can see that the post-war settlement contained an effective balance of fulfilling real immediate needs and promising long term structural changes in

British society. Immediately the settlement, particularly through the Health Service and the education system, met demonstrable basic needs of ordinary people with the costs being socialised. It has become part of the folk law of social policy that the release of pent-up demand for false teeth was difficult to meet. This meeting of immediate needs was balanced both by organisational structures which promised to continue to meet the needs on an ongoing basis and by the promise of structural change in British society whereby disparities of wealth and power, and their concomitant effects on life chances, would progressively diminish.

This settlement contained, second, a vision which combined the personal, the collective, the moral and the material, especially in the notion of citizenship. As citizens, everybody had the duty to contribute to defined individual needs, collectively met, through taxation and, reciprocally, had the right to have these needs met from collective resources. Meeting these needs was divorced from the market and so the personal and the collective were combined with the material and the moral.

This vision may, third, be seen to have both authentic and false components. It was authentic in that it grew from the experiences and needs of ordinary people, it transformed these, and it developed ways in which these needs could be met effectively. The vision was false in that it did not change the material base of the elite enabling their continued domination while adding a new layer of domination. The rise of the welfare state also brought about the rise of professional domination in various forms: the increased definitions of power of the medical profession in the Health Service; the medicalization of increasing numbers of 'social problems'; the birth of new professions such as social work and town planning. All of these, in the name of meeting needs, made the ordinary people subject to increased surveillance and intervention counter to experienced needs. Above all the post-war vision assumed that social justice and capitalist efficiency could be combined into a self-sustaining cycle of economic growth and social reform.

The survival of this vision for some thirty years suggests the power of its meeting of real needs, its promise of structural change and its combination of the personal and the collective, the material and the moral. The demise of this vision may be attributed, in part, to its own internal contradictions, the tension between the authentic and false elements of its vision, brought to a dramatic denouement in the second half of the 1970s. In part the demise of this vision may be traced to the changing place of Britain in the world system: the exhaustion of the industrial base on which the welfare state was predicated; the development (elsewhere) of qualitatively new forms of capitalism based around finance capital and strategies of flexible accumulation.

Thatcherism

It was the crucial weakness of top-down statism of the post-war settlement which Thatcherite populism exploited so effectively in the 1970s and 1980s. The fiscal crises of the 1970s were made a badge that the post-war settlement 'wasn't working'. The alienating experience of people as employees of the state, as patients of the Health Service, as parents of children at school, as users of local government services, and so on, was harnessed by Thatcherism to recruit 'the people' to a crusade by the (new) state against the (old) state. Although there had been some genuine development of a 'public service' ethos, perhaps best seen in the 'universal service' aspirations of the Health Service, the mould was cast in a top-down, Fabian version of state socialism with a heavy emphasis on professionalism and orthodox, hierarchical management. There was very little emphasis on participatory democracy whether employee- or user- based.

This made possible, and at least partially successful, the persistent effort, made by Thatcherism, to denigrate public spending, especially welfare spending, with pejorative attacks on 'bureaucracy', 'scroungers', 'waste', etc. Elements of local, democratic political control were removed or reduced. Public service management structures have been purged with replacements from 'business' or from the heavy use of the party, patronage system. Quasi-market systems of 'contracts' were developed as previous structures were broken up into smaller groups to pursue their own revenue goals.

Above all systematic spending constraints have limited resources in the face of rising demand and need. This consciously aimed at accelerating the growth of private-sector provision. This market growth was structured by the ability to pay and not by needs-based priorities in the context of stagnating or declining standards in the resource-constrained public services. The complexity of the values, policies, manipulation of power over resources involved in shifting the 'frontiers of control' were made apparent by these changes as was, in their denial, the nature and cumulative significance of socialist values, practices and objectives.

One element of irony is that, in practice, Thatcherism was more dictatorially 'state socialist' than any preceding government, as it used the state sector ruthlessly for its own objectives particularly the attempted displacement of the public-service ethos with commercial, competitive and acquisitive norms. It is noteworthy that its programme of subordinating the entire health sector to 'market-contract' type relations, as opposed to shared and linked public-service delivery goals, generated far more bureaucracy and alienation than the old Fabian systems.

In conducting this counter-revolution Thatcherism secured the complicity of very many ordinary people in re-securing their own subordination to the state and in dissipating the productive capital of the local and national state. The 'right' to buy, on favourable terms, the council house that a particular family was renting was a potent weapon which met two objectives: populist support for the primacy of private property; the reduction of local authority housing stocks and the role of local authorities as key suppliers of rented housing. The opportunity of a socially responsible approach which would have allowed both purchase on fair terms and the chance of re-constituting an adequate public housing stock to meet changing social needs was passed up.

The other key example of material, but even more importantly moral complicity in selling off the productive capital of the people, was the privatisation of the nationalised industries. This move was particularly cynical. The government chose to sell in the organisational form that continued the 'monopoly' elements of these vast enterprises but at prices that would allow some windfall gain to small individual purchasers. The reality of ongoing shared ownership was replaced by a temporary, one-off bonus to those joining the process as individual owners. The Treasury maximised its pull on capital wealth and income flows in the process. The economy subsequently suffered from considerable and undesirable price inflation from these newly privatised utilities. The realities are perhaps even more apparent today than they were at the time.

The power of Thatcherism to initiate, and sustain in the medium term, such a counter-revolution derived partially from its simple, total ambition. It proclaimed its radical nature aiming at a fundamental change in British society to make it a service centre for the new epoch of the post-Fordist production of a global capitalism. In proclaiming this Thatcherism sought a cultural revolution both in the sense of changing British culture to fit the perceived new era and in the sense of installing this cultural revolution as a permanent way of life. Management theories about the certainty of uncertainty flourished.

The promise of this new epoch, and the realities of privatisations, enabled Thatcherism to ally disparate groups: high Tories and old working-class Tories could subscribe together with those hoping for meteoric mobility in the services market and the burgeoning class of advisers and consultants oiling the wheels of state restructuring and the Commons Order Papers. The old 'bloc' politics of class-based loyalties was left punching thin air. Forming this coalition depended significantly on a persistent 'splitting' of the field in the stark oppositions of goodies and baddies: dries vs. wets; British vs. foreigners; 'one of us' *versus* 'the enemy within'. Any dissent could be quickly caricatured as polar opposite and thus dismissed, no alternative being available. The metaphors of war, complete with references to 'Winston', pervaded all areas of social policy, and the cynical reality of a war with Argentina enabled an ongoing string of references to nationalism and the treachery of any opposition. These themes articulated with pre-existing elements in British culture creating a new subjectivity combining individualism and familialism with a nationalism, consumerism and, as Hall suggests, a gender-inflected masochism.[2]

This particular combination of themes, idiosyncratic viewed historically and cross-culturally, was coherent enough to offer a vision of individual prosperity and a new stability of perpetual market change for 'middle England'. This was the most interesting and important piece of deception (and perhaps self-delusion). For the processes that Thatcherism set in train pushed more and more of the economic and social system towards dis-equilibrium and cumulative hazard. This is notably so in the case of increased and increasing inequality. In the field of income/employment, Thatcherism reinforced the working of (socially untrammelled) market forces by heavily repressive taxation and by a cumulative legislative pressure to choke off trade union functions and participative rights. It reinforced this further by repealing (or repudiating commitments on) whole generations of legislation protecting the disadvantaged low-paid worker. The cumulative force of all this has been immense and socially corrosive. For instance a limited band of 'normal' working time prevails on the Continent, but here more extreme extension of actual working time exists alongside both structural unemployment and the very

limited hours, and even more limited pay and palpable discrimination against ever larger numbers of part-time workers.

The displacement and exclusion also mounts in a cumulative
way. Thus the younger generation have increasing difficulty in
entering the labour force. Between 1990 and 1994 the number
working full-time under 21 fell by more than half. Of course more
and more youngsters 'stayed on' or went into Further or Higher
Education; but the number of teaching professionals in full-time
work who should be supporting this shift to longer education
actually fell by 10 per cent between 1991-1994. But the statistics
also show a massive reduction in the numbers in full-time work in
their 50s. There is more to displacement than the official unemployed figures. The crisis of young people, and its profound effects
on family structures and expectations, is the antithesis of the
'opportunity' and family-centred values of Thatcherite rhetoric. For
a few years, Thatcherism manipulated 'feel good' factors perhaps
for the majority; but the disruptive and violently inegalitarian
commercialism it has unleashed and reinforced not only no longer
affects only a minority, but is oppressively visible to the majority.
Schumpeter characterised the dynamism of capitalist economies as
'creative destruction'. Thatcherism is practice has reinforced the
destructive aspects. Whereas earlier in the post-war period our
'mixed economies' and 'welfare' states developed elements of
social justice and recognition of shared needs to produce some
periods of balance and stability (precariously, as we now recognise), Thatcherism attacked the very elements (the 'social wage';
accumulation of socially controlled capital; some progressive
re-distribution) that might produce a socially tolerable mixture of
risk and creativity with social concern and solidarity. In doing so
it has reaped the whirlwind – but so have the British people.

Nevertheless the attempted counter-revolution (for that was
what it was) was far from complete. We are still quite far from the
dissipation of 'socialised' resources, material and moral, and their
dis-integration into market and profit centred ones which the
Thatcherite ideologues were still desperately pursuing while they
still had power – though very little legitimacy. This is not just
a matter of say, Scottish water, of nuclear power, or of railway
services. In the utility sector, even while they 'sold the family
silver', they had to develop systems of public regulation which
open the dialogue between market forces and the public interest
in new forms, some of them more 'open' than the formal accountability of the old state monoliths. Nor did they dissolve the almost

instinctive loyalty of masses of ordinary people to the value systems of social justice (fairness and universal access) in education and health; thus, in 'middle' England the social solidarity of parents, teachers, governors and local government/communities over education services and government cuts is quite simply a revelation. Nor did they convert the professional cadres involved, though management specialists, eg accountants, have been more pliable – and more heavily bribed with 'rewards'.

Thus there is an element in Thatcherite rhetoric that may have more positive significance. Thatcherism raised a banner for consumer interests. The argument was that liberating the competitive market would ensure consumer well-being in the commercial sectors, but the consumer should be empowered in the areas of state monopoly and bureaucracy. This in practice ranged between diluting local government control of schools and offering instead more parental control (governors), and the very limited agenda opened up by the idea of the 'consumers charter' in public services. There are actually potentially constructive elements in this. Theology, especially Catholic theology, has been suspicious or hostile in its approach to consumerism which it assumes as selfish and this-worldly in its demands. But our needs-based public services have too often substituted professional interpretation of need for the actual voices and concerns of users, young and old. Developing representative capacity for the needs of the disadvantaged, offering participation in the detailed development of, say, state education, is as likely to be a long-term exercise in the development of social responsibility for consumers as well as for producers. Thatcherism offered little more than a fudge; but increasingly radical, often community-centred, consumer groups are already asking for more dialogue rather than vestigial consultation. The value system of socially responsible consumer-based organisation is something that needs more examination. How then does the Thatcherite vision fare when addressed by the three questions specified at the beginning of the chapter?

First, Thatcherism offers a sense of both the end of history and an ever-unrolling horizon. As with Fukayama the final, inevitable form of human society is heralded as now present (bar the minor details of reforming institutional relics). This essentially static vision is given movement, even manic movement, by the offer of individual social mobility; those individuals willing and able to meet the demands of the ever-changing market may hope for unlimited advance, materially conceived. Thatcherism, conversely, contains a powerful method for dealing with disillusion; those for whom the horizons do not unfurl are personally responsible for their failure to conform to the demands of the market.

This vision contains, second, a distinctive combination of the personal and the collective, the moral and the material. The personal, the moral and the material combine in the ethic of enlightened self-interest; pursuing personal material advantage becomes, through the 'hidden hand' of the market, the privileged, even the only, way in which the moral society is established, while individual morality is left open within the strict limits of social discipline. The role of the collective is restricted to creating and maintaining the conditions for the pursuit of individual self-interest, particularly social discipline.

This vision offers, we suggest, false hope. While the promise of individual social mobility in a middle-class permanent revolution has proved to be a powerful electoral incentive, its offer is ultimately unsustainable. The restriction of the collective to matters of social discipline misrepresents the essentially social, and necessarily co-operative, nature of material production and distribution. The perfect market of liberal economic theory never exists, not so much because of imperfect competition as because non-market-based social processes always intrude at the heart of production and distribution. The 'rationality' of the market is always, necessarily, underpinned by collaborative relations antithetical to competition. The Thatcherite vision can be seen to offer false hope in other ways. The offer of hope for ongoing social mobility through market competition is necessarily a zero-sum game – the fulfilment of one person's hopes are at the expense of the denial of the hopes of another. Failure and disillusion are structural necessities of the Thatcherite vision. Containing this disillusion invokes an increasingly intrusive and oppressive set of state controls on personal life thus rendering its version of hope untenable. As we suggested in Chapter 1 both the contented and the dispossessed are trapped by the culture of contentment on which Thatcherism depends: the former by fear of the future, the latter by absence of hope.

Notes to Chapter 3

1. Raymond Williams: *Drama from Ibsen to Brecht* (Harmonsworth: Penguin Books Ltd, 1973).
2. Stuart Hall: *The Hard Road to Renewal: Thatcherism and the Crisis of the Left* (London: Verso, 1988).

PART TWO

From Past to Present: Claiming Traditions

INTRODUCTION

✳

W E have expounded our understanding of the nature of hope, shown the signs of its withering in Britain and similar 'end of history' societies, and analysed the two most recent versions of hopeful vision in Britain, with their strengths and weaknesses.

We now turn to an exposition of tradition, in the conviction that hope as a bringing-together of the present and the future is also derived from the past or – to put it another way – that the process of vision-formation can, and probably must, draw on resources of the living past. We do not start from nowhere; we live within traditions.

Our emphasis on the transcendent and transformative nature of hope does not imply a denial of our belonging within a history which shapes not only our circumstances and conditions but also our perceptions and understandings.

We have just been examining our immediate historical context, namely in the last half-century in this country. We now extend the historical perspective to an inheritance which is both long and broader, namely to two major traditions – the socialist and the Christian. Few would deny that the Christian tradition has been a long and influential one in this region of the world, whereas there would be less agreement about the length and strength of the influence of socialism. Our case for choosing to examine these two traditions as resources for vision formation is that both are significantly influential traditions (though not of equal influence), that both use the language of hope and vision in a way that is congruent with our convictions, and that they have been in con-siderable interaction with one another, not least in Britain whether in cooperation or in confrontation, in assimilation or in antipathy. It will already be apparent from our exposition of hope that our understanding is heavily influenced by Judaeo-Christian writings, not least those of the Christian canon.

But first we need to define tradition more carefully and expound our understanding of how to relate creatively to it.

Tradition seems a fairly dead hand to lay on a project which is concerned with social vision for the future, and it may well not sound promising to announce that we intend to draw upon or speak from particular traditions. Much of the sectarianism of both Christianity and socialism has been fuelled by appeals to the 'authentic' tradition, passionately debating esoteric points of doctrine to the consternation of 'outsiders', and even to speak of tradition may be felt to inhibit public debate by limiting vision for the future to the reproduction of the past or by excluding those who don't belong to the tradition. Furthermore, both traditions contain much that current adherents would be glad to disown (conspicuously, the excesses of the Inquisition and of Stalinism).

All of which makes us wary of getting trapped in sterile debate. Yet we believe that we all speak, almost inevitably, from our own various traditions, and that as Christians or as socialists we make our most valid contribution to public debate when we speak consciously and explicitly from our traditions. Not that these are monolithic. It is not our case that the whole weight of Christian or socialist tradition points in a particular direction for Scotland at the end of the twentieth century, nor that the elements upon which we draw are the authentic tradition and all others distortions or impostors. Rather we believe that there are elements in the traditions on which we can draw to enrich the debate.

By tradition we mean not only a varied heritage of thinking, but a range (over time and place) of practice, and an ongoing community formed by and re-forming that thinking and practice. Our attempt to draw on the traditions is therefore an attempt to speak from where (and who) we are. We reflect on the tensions and antinomies within the traditions, and are aware that other threads than those we emphasise might have been drawn on (and might point in other directions). Our choice, however, is not entirely eclectic; it comes partly from a loyalty to the traditions as dynamic and participative and plural (and therefore open rather than closed); it comes partly from an honest attempt to see which strands in the traditions might have most to contribute to building a social vision in Scotland today, and so, crucially, it comes out of an engagement with the contemporary scene. We are not seeking in the past either theoretically or in practice the blueprint to which we must return; rather we are hoping for a 'fusion of horizons' in which participation in change within the present context interacts with elements in the tradition to reform each other.

This is not easy in a climate where visionaries and pragmatists have learned mutual mistrust (witness current signs of strife between 'old' and 'new' Labour), and academic theoreticians and community activists don't listen to each other long enough to have much of a common language. We attempted to bridge this gap in a small-scale listening exercise with some community activists in Easterhouse in Glasgow. What emerged was far from a battalion of politically-motivated people inspired by a vision to get involved in community change; rather, we found a lively network of folk starting by reacting passionately to felt injustice, determining to do something about that and gradually getting involved in wider issues. When, prompted, they spoke of vision or motivation, what came over were elements from Christian and (to a lesser extent) socialist tradition embedded in a wider culture and becoming a vital part of people most of whom would run from either label.

Their engagement with their community, especially in its powerful perception and experience of injustice, as well as in its crucial hope, is as basic to our project as engagement with the traditions, but the two cannot be exclusive. They must become interactive. Standing where we are, in the context of 1990s Britain, we draw on our traditions for inspiration; standing where we are, in the context of our traditions, we engage with what's going on in our communities.

Having briefly outlined (earlier in this study) an understanding of where Britain stood in 1997, we therefore take a critical look at these two major traditions, to see what can be contributed from them towards an animating and liberating social vision. To a greater or lesser extent we see these traditions as authoritative, recognising them as bearers of truth, but would argue that such a view does not restrict debate to those who can accept the Westminster Confession, papal infallibility, or whatever; rather it represents a rich resource and a valid contribution we can make to a highly plural debate. That is, not because we have sole copyright on the truth, but because our traditions embody crucial aspects of that public truth. They are themselves plural and constantly changing.

Traditions which are not closed are hard to define, and it is beyond our scope to attempt either definition or comprehensive review; we are not attempting to defend or vindicate either tradition, but hope to draw out those strands which seem to offer the most creative interaction with the present scene. Thus the traditions can be seen as dynamic, creating their own new forms, in interaction with each other, with other traditions and with their social contexts. This happens at different levels – of anthropology or world-views, of values, of insights, of practical projects – in the process of vision-building.

So we approach these two major traditions, both highly influential in Scottish culture though both challenged by some as to whether they have a continuing relevance. In fact, our starting point for this project lies at least to some extent in the alleged end of the socialist tradition in the collapse of its actually existing form in eastern Europe around 1990. In reviewing that tradition, our case will be that there are elements cherished and nurtured within it which still have much to contribute; in reviewing Christian tradition, we will also draw out threads that can be fruitfully part of rebuilding a wider social vision in a Scotland which may, in large measure, have forsaken the Kirk but not its values. We do not uncover a holy grail, but a story, or rather stories, in the hermeneutic of which a vision may emerge.

CHAPTER 4

Varieties
of Socialist Tradition

THERE are whole libraries of books which hack away at this great mountain of movements and ideas. For example, Max Beer's two volumes on *British Socialism* give a patient and honest survey of earlier socialist tradition in this particular part of the globe. What limited review is offered here has four purposes.

First, to recognise the historical conditioning of both thought and movements, and therefore the need for both 'revision' and 'renaissance' of earlier socialist reflection and aspiration as the dynamic of economic and social development pushes fresh opportunities and social tensions at us.

Second, to reflect on the tensions and opposed positions *within* the socialist traditions, tensions relating both to values and analysis and to strategies of social action. These conflicts of principle and practice include questions of organisational forms of socialist movements and of actual – or would-be – socialist societies, as well as questions about modes of empowerment.

Third, to raise some of the issues arising from 'really existent' socialism, both in what were self-declared socialist countries, and in 'mixed' economies such as the UK.

Fourthly, to ask what creative borrowing might be indulged in, in today's circumstances, or whether some of the traditional categories can no longer carry the responses now called for.

Forerunners

A brief flashback to early vestiges of the socialist tradition shows that, though industrial and commercial capitalism stimulated socialist thought and movements, traces of socialism emerge for millennia before that. If socialism is something more than an oppositional response to capitalism in various nineteenth and twentieth century versions, it may be a movement of ideas that looks back for its inspiration as well as *forward*.

As an early instance we catch a glimpse of what is palpably socialist thought through the sharply satirical treatment of Aristophanes in his play *The Ecclesiazusae* (or Women in Council):

Praxagora[1]:   *I want all to have a share of everything and all property to be in common: there will no longer be either rich or poor; no longer shall we see one man harvesting vast tracts of land, while another has not ground enough to be buried in ...*

I shall begin by making land, money, everything that is private property, common to all. Then we shall live on this common wealth, which we shall take care to administer with wise thrift.

Common ownership, as a theme here, carries phrasing that seems to echo in, for instance, the recently abandoned working of Clause 4 in the Labour Party's constitution. But Aristophanes in 412 BC interlocked that challenge on property rights with issues of women's role and rights (thereby touching another modern fault line in the socialist tradition). If socialist ideas emerge in classical Athens within a city-state of commerce and private property endemically trapped in inter-state wars, they almost certainly hark back as well as proposing to innovate; they may well draw on earlier human experience of shared resources and common property within the tribal group in neolithic and pre-neolithic societies, and on matriarchy.

A further early instance is the sudden flame of socialist sharing, and distribution according to need, at the beginning of a different kind of ecclesia. With the first appearance of the 'believers' immediately after the death of Jesus there is the ineradicable image in Acts 2: 44ff and Acts 4: 32 of the believers having all things in common and dividing their goods according to need.

This response, however transient it may have been, links the socialist and the Christian traditions *ab initio*. These were, after all, the people closest in time and place to Jesus. If the message was that you may partake in common and with equal regard in things incorruptible, why not seek to practice such mutual respect and aid in the things corruptible of daily living? Nor can such sharing be viewed as sectarian. The congregations that grew from these first 'believers' were far from seeing themselves in any exclusive way as 'the chosen'. They were on the edge of one of the most important of all religious breakthroughs, opening the message out from within the Jewish faith to all humanity.

In the Middle Ages the idea of socialism is particularly linked to village communities and to collective elements in their agrarian practice. Max Beer, in his volumes on *British Socialism*, devotes his first section to 'medieval communism'.[2] Those 'roots' of socialism developing from medieval society drew strength from an egalitarian criticism of society and hierarchy derived from Christian traditions, but they were also rooted in actual experience. Village communities, as they emerged from the dark ages (and as they persisted in much of Britain – and in diverse but related forms across much of Europe – through a thousand years of the regulated 'open field' system) exercised – and struggled to defend and maintain – elements of shared social control. These related to shared management of the agrarian system through collective supervision of land use, grazing and livestock, boundaries *etc*, carrying both responsibilities and rights.

The brilliant and evocative socialist advocacy of Gerard Winstanley, writing and attempting direct action during the English civil war, was in social practice divisive. For he raised the awkward question of the rights of *all* to use and develop common land, when those common rights that were in practical operation represented the claims and accepted usage of the local community.

Those elements of 'common' rights shared by the local community persisted and were socially educative over many centuries. When eventually that community organisation was fractured in the eighteenth and early nineteenth centuries by the imposition of capitalist farming, it is not surprising that so much experience of collective organisation and mutuality was re-worked in co-operative organisation and philosophy of many kinds. Expropriation of that persistent community control, particularly through enclosure (an important aspect of what Marx termed the 'primitive accumulation' on which capitalism was built), had to use the sovereign power of an unrepresentative Parliament to override the 'common' elements of local community control. Enclosure could be triggered by manipulated voting – in this case by proportion of land owned, rather than number of proprietors; the professional 'commissioners' who oversaw the complex re-allocation of land might be seen as forerunners of the regulators now supervising 'privatised' utilities.

Coming to the last of our forerunners, Babeuf, in the aftermath of the French Revolution, spoke and struggled for an egalitarian socialism which challenged the extreme inequalities that lay behind the 'constitutional equality' of bourgeois society. Advocating a 'Republic of Equals' at his trial before his execution in 1797, he held that 'The Jacobins failed to obtain Social Equality; therefore we must have Communism'; so he argued for:

> *The common good or the community of goods! No more private property in land .... We claim the common use of the fruits of the earth .... Let there be for all one education and one standard of life!*

The Secret Directory of his proscribed movement adopted a manifesto saying:

> *The end of society is to defend ... an equal right to the enjoyment of all the goods of life ... and to augment, by the co-operation of all, the common enjoyments of all .... There is oppression wherever one part of society is exhausted by labour and in want ... whilst the other part wallows in abundance without doing any work at all .... No one can, by accumulating to himself the means, deprive another of the instruction necessary for his happiness. Instruction ought to be common to all.*

We seem to be back with Praxagora in 412 BC, but these words were translated by Bronterre O'Brien, the Chartist, and the special emphasis on 'one education' takes us straight into contemporary controversy.

Some Tensions between different Schools of Socialist Thought and Practice

We start with the familiar distinction between 'utopian' and Marxist or 'scientific' socialism; the 1848 Communist Manifesto quite deliberately chose to force this distinction forward. The criticism of the 'utopians' was that developing their systems of thought in an early ('undeveloped') stage of capitalism, they could not identify the developing 'material' conditions for the 'emancipation' of working people, and instead 'invented' new patterns of organisation of society; future history becomes for them 'the propaganda and practical application of their plans'. In particular, the 'utopians', instead of sharing in the 'gradual and spontaneous organisation of the proletariat as a class', try to take a position above 'class antagonism and endeavour by experiments and example to prepare the way for their 'social gospel'.

There is some force in such a criticism. The various experiments in 'communities' represented in many cases a separating-off or withdrawal from the commercial society. They faced problems of longer-term adjustment, since society and its organisation was highly dynamic, and their community structures might tend to the static; they also had still to learn how to deal with the 'outside' world.

There are some deep historic ironies here. For the Marxist critics generated movements which took power, in the name of socialist doctrines, in highly 'undeveloped' societies/economies. *Their* subsequent 'experiments' could be distinguished from the utopians' only in terms of vast scale and involuntary and coercive adoption of the new forms; there was an astonishing similarity between the organisational system of Owenite agricultural or craft-skilled communes and that of revolutionary Maoism in China in the 1960s. And the 'really existent' economies failed in many ways to match the dynamic technological sweep, and innovation in products and services, of mature capitalism; that emulative comparison with the 'outside' world was one dimension of the defeat of their practice.

But there were other dimensions to the utopians' practice: organisation and influence within the capitalist environment. Of course, success and subsequent failure or loss of momentum were historically conditioned, but they were nevertheless important. Take consumer co-operation, which at one stage had its highest share of retail distribution in Scotland; it did not require daunting capital sums for its operation; it secured and passed on some useful economies of scale; an early trump card was that it could offer products that were not deliberately adulterated; it generated habits of collective self-government, rights and responsibilities; it offered an element of 'saving' in the hands of working-class women (the dividend); it linked local societies into federated movements; it also developed mutuality in building societies and insurance. Philanthropic concern added the extraordinarily widespread development of 'friendly societies', through supportive legislation, encapsulating the principles of mutuality and democratic government. So socialist habits and practice were experienced by large numbers of working-class people over several generations, building elements of the 'co-operative commonwealth'. The analogy with 'the Kingdom' may be worth pondering. It is not a disproof of the social relevance of socialist principles that some of these forms of co-operative organisation in

Britain have lost ground to capital-rich and technologically advanced commercial rivals, as witness the current bribing of members of 'mutual' building societies to sell their rights in return for what to them are substantial capital sums. As to retail societies, John Hughes and Sidney Pollard tried to persuade the co-operatives in the late 1950s to develop a powerful multiple organisation in place of the old area-based societies – another 'utopian' might-have-been.

As to the Marxist-influenced strands of socialist thought and organisation, it would be wrong to underrate their intellectual grasp of the dynamic and the crisis-ridden development-path of modern capitalism. Indeed, the best twentieth century work on business-cycles and 'accumulation' theories has come from writers heavily influenced by Marx. However it is strange that the Marxist studies of the transition of feudal (and traditional) societies to commercial capitalist relations emphasised the long drawn-out and complex processes by which capitalist forms of enterprise and relationships developed within the old 'integuments', whereas the projection of the transition from capitalism to socialism was seen to proceed out of 'crisis' into revolutionary confrontation and overthrow. This was a dramatically 'apocalyptic' scenario, but imposed deep problems of the credibility and management of such a process. Thus, there was virtually no expectation that both individuals and communities would have at least partial experience of organisation aimed at meeting social need rather than profit, or that principles of socialised evaluation of development needs would enjoy some potency for some time.

This led to an over-emphasis on the role of 'class' movements and 'class' organisation in the anticipated revolutionary process, and therefore to advocacy and practice of 'adversarial' action, eg by trade unions, almost as an end-in-itself. It also meant there was very little prior conception of the measures that might be taken in the name of socialist construction. One danger of the revolutionary assumption was the emphasis on discipline, authoritarianism, and centralism. The initial measures set out in the Manifesto in 1848 were sketchy in the extreme: abolition of property in land and of inheritance; centralisation in the hands of 'the state' of credit and 'the means of transport'; extension of national factories; obligation of all to labour; 'organisation of industrial armies'; free public education for all children. This was not much more detailed than Babeuf, and seems hardly to relate to the emphasis on understanding the real economic nature of capitalism. It can hardly escape the criticism that it is in turn what was criticised as 'utopian' ('social activity is to be replaced by their personal inventive activity').

A further deep division in socialist advocacy and analysis is to be found in the contrast between state-socialist thinking and communitarian or anarchist (and related) schools of thought. This division of opinion cuts across the reformist *versus* revolutionary contrast. State socialists, *eg* of the British 'Fabian' tradition, might sound gradualist and reformist, in contrast to the 'revolutionary' Marxism quoted above. Community-based advocacy might, as with nineteenth century anarchism, have explicitly revolutionary expectations and tactics.

It could be said without too much oversimplification that instead of questioning the form and jurisdiction of the state, state socialists looked to taking over its sovereignty, whether by democratic or by other means. For the most part they also emphasised the distinctive 'sovereignty' of property rights; hence the over-emphasis on changing private into public property, with the assumption that this high significance of property rights would continue. In addition, on this basis the state socialist assumed the continuation of the propertied employer-wage-employee relationship.

The alternative, communitarian or quasi-anarchist, traditions at least challenged segments of the state-socialist vision. The anarchist tradition placed particular emphasis on local 'community', whether village or city, and looked for its participative self-development – usually on the basis of restoration of much relevant property to community control, and a sharing that related both to contribution and to needs. In particular the anarchist directly challenged the authoritarian 'sovereign' claims of 'state' authority, which it linked with legitimation of the use of force in social relationships; it looked instead to a network of co-operative or federated links between communities.

The state socialist position was also sharply contested by syndicalist thought, which sought to replace capitalist management by that of the workers, very much through a transformation of the role of industrial trade unions. A more sophisticated approach, to which G. D. H. Cole greatly contributed, evolved the concept of the operation of industry by 'guilds' (note the conscious harking back) of workers whose self-government and industrial responsibilities would be based on some kind of franchising or equivalent relation (one might think of 'licensing') with the state as 'owner'. In the last-mentioned point of view there is at least a significant shift away from assuming that whoever 'owns' the property would have sweeping powers over its disposal or use. Interestingly, the First International at its meeting in Brussels in 1868 came up with some similar notions to the 'guild' socialists:

> ... we see in the trade unions the embryos of the great workers' companies which will one day replace the capitalist companies ... they will be organised equitably, founded on mutuality and justice.

and concerning mines, oil wells, and railways:

> ... would belong to the social body as a whole, represented by the State, ... (but) they will be conceded by society to workers' companies, in virtue of a double contract ... guaranteeing to society the scientific and rational exploitation of the concession ... as near as possible at cost price (with) the right to inspect the Company's books ... ; on the other hand guaranteeing the mutual rights of each member of the workers' Association.[3]

The problem for both systems of thought – the state-socialist and the syndicalist or guild-socialist – is that they both take a relatively *static* view of the notion of industry or sector, which can be a trap in the longer term (cf the coal industry). They also seem inclined to concentrate on 'massed' organisation with a likely high degree of monopoly power (this was explicit in the organisation of British nationalised industries). There are problems as to the effective recognition and representation of consumer interests within both approaches, though this is much less true if public ownership stems from local government.

There are a whole series of real world difficulties in the conventional state-socialist approach:

First, if anything, the approach relied on, assumed, and sought to take over a claim to a high degree of *sovereign* power. This should have been seen as more of a problem in British socialism earlier in the twentieth century when that power was massively imperialist. More widely, there is an assumption of military power (force) which was seldom adequately addressed. In the current European context this must seem obsolete, and the issues of interdependence, shared sovereignty, and the recognition of the contexts and issues for which significant abrogation of sovereignty is required are much more openly addressed.

Second, state socialist thinking and practice all too readily involved a centralising emphasis that was also likely to involve substantial routinisation and bureaucracy. This might have seemed least harmful in some utilities such as nineteenth century postal systems or services such as railways where long-lived capital could offer nationally-linked services. Much of the 1945 government's nationalisation was concerned with such 're-organisation', *eg* of electricity. But the approach produces problems when technology and product and process innovation become fast moving. Besides there was an evident disinclination to pass state economic organisation and control *down* to regions and communities (ironically, in this sense Thatcherism was intensely state-socialist).

Third, there was a trap also in the conventional emphasis on the *power* of property rights, and the emphasis on transferring this (absolute) power to the state only confirmed that emphasis. This did little to resolve the more complex issues/opportunities involved in developing (and ensuring) responsible use of property, in developing the participation in property-based decisions (*eg* on development) of other major groups in society (social partners, consumer interests, community representatives), and in stimulating creative experiment in working methods and relationships. In the eastern bloc, state industrial property was operated with scant concern for the environmental costs and the damage inflicted on communities and on workers.

Finally, in British experience of this emphasis on nationalised monopolies within a still substantially capitalist economy, two further real world problems became apparent in practice. One was that in the name of the 'national interest' there was actually subservience to the interests of UK capitalist suppliers of equipment, and users of the nationalised industry's end product. The other was that the management of pricing policy, the timing and extent of capital spending and borrowing, became increasingly subject to Treasury manipulation, motivated by concerns as to short-run management of the economy. The public enterprises did not lead, they followed, and deferred to other powerful interests. The potential of more rational and socially responsible use of public property was not achieved.

In the context of criticism of state socialism it is proper to give honourable mention to Hilaire Belloc's warning analysis in *The Servile State* (editions from 1912 to 1927). His argument was that capitalist states, partly under the pressure of state-socialist demands and advocacy, were not actually approaching socialism but rather a very different society, a 'servile state'. As he saw it, a capitalist class (with hindsight one might add – and/or a managerial class) in such a state would be even more powerful and secure, but the 'proletarian mass' would 'change their status, lose their present legal freedom, and be subject to compulsory labour'. He saw compulsory insurance, 'registration, and control of the proletariat' as leading to 'a fatal approach to compulsory labour'. Instead, therefore, of emphasis on the use of the powers of compulsion of the nation state, he argued for a 'distributive' solution, sharing power and resources, encouraging independence and initiative.

Belloc's argument has considerable force. The replacing both of more or less 'liberal' capitalism and of 'emancipating' socialist goals and practice by authoritarian 'statism' across much of Europe for long periods in the twentieth century has been a reality few foresaw when Belloc wrote. The fascism that suppressed independent working-class organisation, and went on to forced labour and direction of labour, and the state 'socialism' that did the same over protracted periods, fit Belloc's argument all too well.

The increasingly authoritarian overtones of UK Conservative governments in recent years point down the same road to social disaster. This is apparent not only in the cumulative legal constraints on trade union functions and the non-acceptance of European minimum standards and rights for workers, but also in incentives to employers to offer ultra-low wages with extending state subsidisation means-tested to the recipient worker. These are, in economic reality, a free gift to the employer which combine with increased compulsion on the unemployed to accept work on adverse terms or lose benefit and with Orwellian displacement of language (the unemployed disappear from the official vocabulary and become job-seekers). But in this latest state of UK governance there is not even the will or capacity to provide work for all. In this society there is ample reason to reach back to the socialist tradition in its many varieties in the search for alternatives that carry respect for those in need.

Underlying Values

In this socialist tradition or variety of traditions, ethical language and efforts to build systems, programmes, and responses to social and economic pressures in terms of 'principle', figure prominently. It would be a massive task to analyse and appraise these value systems; besides, because of the wide range of social and historical conditions involved, there must be genuine problems of interpretation and understanding. What follows is therefore tentative and substantially conditioned by being written at this 'moment in time', both in its concerns and in its attempt to distil lessons from 'hindsight'.

We distinguish three groupings of socialist values. We do not suggest that they represent a hierarchy of values; we recognise that there are questions of balance and sometimes of tension between the three. We are not dealing with absolutes which dictate the course of action but with debatable choice within the 'language of priorities'.

The three groups of values relate firstly to social solidarity, secondly to social justice, linked with egalitarian principles, and thirdly to creativity, freedom and self-determination. The order chosen, while not implying a hierarchy, indicates a sense of the cumulative distinctiveness of the concerns. It will be clear that there is an echo of the dominant slogan of the French revolution's three sound-bites − *Liberte, Egalite, Fraternite*.

Social Solidarity

The emphasis on social solidarity and its requirements suggests common ground with the Christian exhortation to love of neighbour. However, the socialist emphasis is on co-operative, shared activity and in particular, in contrast to commercially-dominated capitalist systems, it emphasises the values of mutuality and support in place of emulative competition.

Of course, the organisational forms and associated ethos of social solidarity are historically conditioned. The solidarity which they express is evidently related in many cases to what the 'solidarist' group is struggling against; thus the collectivism of wage workers coming together in trade unions is (in part, but only in part) directed against the imbalance of power between employer − which today may mean global corporation − and individual employee. But the moral processes involved cannot simply be subsumed in issues of power and social struggle.

Group solidarity carries the risk of turning in on itself and excluding others. But the thrust of socialist solidarity has been a turning out, a widening of the practice and concerns of solidarity; co-operative organisation, both of consumers and in many industries, has shown this capacity to extend the scope of mutual support globally. Trade unions have learnt to mediate between the interests of different groups of workers, and again to widen both organisation and accepted responsibilities. In both cases, federation rather than formal hierarchy has characterised their linkages.

The emphasis on responsible participation within these solidarist structures is also significant; they involve active sharing rather than passive representation. The practice of solidarity can be a powerful force in the development and social learning of those involved, and with it the widening of agendas and purposes, and the opening out of the answer to the question 'who is my neighbour'.

The 'universalist' element in the value-systems of social solidarity may have a new charge of energy in today's world. Information technology enables the connections and communications of global sharing. Interdependence, in economic and social terms, keeps breaking beyond conventional commercial 'market' forms. Environmental concerns and responsibilities present an extending agenda, which is only manageable by acceptance of the value-norms of social solidarity. The questions both of shared and sustainable resources and of participation and accountability in the process concerned pull heavily and persistently towards the values and potential practice of social solidarity. Market aggrandisement, hierarchies of non-accountable power, blindness to wider social costs and benefits in pursuit of commercial gain, a greedy and aggressive individualism – these can no more offer practical solutions than they can offer moral alternatives to the creative pursuit of social solidarity.

Social Justice

When Adam delved and Eve span,
Who was then the gentleman?

It is hardly necessary to re-work the arguments for equality that have played so consistent a role in socialist thought. Nor can the centrality of the moral issues involved be avoided in an increasingly unequal society and economy, set in a dramatically unequal world. Cumulative deprivation exists alongside extremes of individual 'wealth'. The linked questions of 'just' distribution and opportunities for the full development of all change little in ethical terms, but practical means and objectives have continually to be re-thought. But what *is* the proper scope of considerations of social justice and egalitarianism in the socialist tradition? May the demand for social justice become distorted in practice, or swallow up other ethical concerns?

One of the first matters to take up is that of the key areas of application for social justice. An inescapable starting point is that of the meeting of 'basic needs'. This has to be thought of in dynamic terms, not only in the sense that we are concerned with the requirements for human *development*, but also because in some areas (especially information/communication) innovation has a transforming role. For example, universal access to telecommunications services is being debated across Europe as the European Commission is treating it as a required concomitant of 'liberalised' telecom markets; but the reality of 'basic' access to telecommunications is itself in rapid development.

Of course, important areas of 'need' are met, at least in substantial part, in a wide range of modern states (our own included) by collective provision and expenditure. Though the boundaries shift, we may distinguish between provision of such needs according to need (social as well as individual) without subjecting the use to market-price mechanisms, and those which are handled by modifying the outcomes of particular markets so that more socially-identified needs are met (than would have been the case without intervention). For examples of the former (which we might term 'communal' as against 'market' delivery) we can take familiar categories such as public educational and health services, many amenity services including most roads, and public security services. For examples of the latter, a wide range of public utility services (including transport, water, energy, telecoms) where intervention (through public ownership and/or regulation) affects the 'affordability' of universal services as well as the quality and range of services. Housing is a particularly sensitive example, with public intervention both in housing provision (*eg* 'social housing' in various forms) and manipulation of tax/benefit to supplement income or subsidise housing costs.

The issues of social justice in these matters are complex, far-reaching, and contested, within the socialist tradition as well as outside it. Determination of 'need' and provision for needs is one dimension of ethical concern. One question is how far professional interests (*eg* in health, education, or indeed in security services) distort outcome and their resource costs. Another issue is the scale of provision (and therefore choices as to resource allocation) not least in a 'mixed' economy; thus, constrained or 'rationed' provision of needed services (as for instance in education or in health) on a communal basis might stimulate – indeed, might be designed to stimulate – unequal provision delivered through the market. Moreover, the financing of needs-based services is likely to rest on taxation, direct and indirect, which may not fully respect 'ability to pay' or progressive contribution norms.

A decisively important area of social justice is access to 'work' and the requirement to contribute to society through work. The earlier socialist traditions were quite sharp on the latter point (he who does not work, neither shall he eat), but were perhaps less helpful in the matter of the *balance* between work, self-development outside work, recreation, participation in social action and decisions, within the context of prolonged life expectation. The elements of social justice involved in access to work and in its 'fair' remuneration are no less complex than in health or education. The moral intuition of the socialist tradition is undoubtedly one for the provision of work for all, but for work that is socially constructive and offers some degree of individual fulfilment. In the mixed economy this requires a continuing redefinition of the societal and human responsibilities of commercial enterprise, which is no mean task in face of quasi-commercial value systems that treat labour more as cost than resource and the displacement effect of development as achievement rather than as a moment in a continuing commitment to include people and their communities rather than exclude them. It also calls for a fresh recognition that the 'communal' sectors of the economy and society can find more socially-beneficial work to do if there is the social commitment forthcoming to manage the income transfers and efficient husbanding of resources that may be involved.

Even these manifold issues do not cover the dilemmas involved in pressing the moral imperative of social justice. Some of these dilemmas should at least be delineated.

First, the word 'imperative' may be more evident than the sense of moral commitment. Thus, pursuit of social justice may reinforce a 'state power' approach to socialist goals; rights, re-distribution, justice, may be too heavily reliant on the authoritative and coercive use of legislative and administrative power and on the degree of uniformity that may go with it.

Second, there can be an unresolved tension between one country's felt needs and claims and those of other countries. This may point towards deployment of social-justice concerns within wider federalist frameworks, and with international commitments and institutions involved in sharing and redistributing resources and in raising minimum standards of social rights and responsibilities.

Third, questions of just distribution and access to resources need to be set in a long-term context. Justice as between successive generations is an unavoidable moral dimension; in contemporary terms the question of 'sustainable' resources and their scope for growth, together with the distributional implications, is a crucial element in the ethics of social justice. Bertrand Russell grasped this when he wrote, eighty years ago,

> *The purpose of maximising production will not be achieved in the long run if our present industrial system continues. Our present system is wasteful of human material .... The same is true of material resources: the minerals, the virgin forests, and the newly developed wheatfields of the world are being exhausted with a reckless prodigality which represents almost a certainty of hardship for future generations.*[4]

It is not only that a substantial part of so-called wealth generation in the twentieth century has been based on once-for-all extraction and robbery of global resources; it is also that much consumption has been accompanied by high social costs of pollution and other environmental damage. This means that, even if democratic majorities in 'advanced' countries might will it, they cannot with any moral force seek to level up for all to the style and standards of living of the wealthier citizens. This certainly conflicts with the Kantian principle that moral actions should be capable of being universalised. It must also be evident that socialist concerns with social justice require a transformed degree of social responsibility from industrial and commercial enterprises, whether they are, in formal legal terms, social or public institutions or joint-stock or private partnerships.

Creativity and Freedom

The third emphasis within the socialist canon, namely on creativity, has sometimes been more implicit than explicit, though for some key figures in British socialist thought it was central: one might instance William Morris with his concern with transforming work and its scope for artistic creativity, and Bertrand Russell who saw it in even wider categories of intellectual challenge. Openness to experiment, innovation, varieties of social experience goes hand in hand with free expression. The critique of capitalist relations had time and again concentrated on its repression and distortion of work, on its denial of creativity and self-determination in wage work, and more directly (cf the Webbs) on capitalism as dictatorship.

It has to be asked why much of the attempted socialism in practice appears as a retreat from such central concern with these principles of creativity and freedom. This is not the place for an appraisal of the emergence of repression or uniformity and routinisation. Both revolutionary and reformist socialist practice have contributed to those. The classic critique of socialist parties in practice (Michels' *Political Parties*) was, after all, published before 1914; its 'iron law' of oligarchy was all too fully documented; the current 'new' patterns of 'leadership' in the British Labour Party seem to come direct from its pages. As to the lack of creativity in the British attempts at large-scale public ownership, these owed much to taking over sectors heavily dependent on routinisation in their systems before the liberating advent of computers for such tasks. They owed still more to a deferential following of conventional management practice from large-scale capitalist firms (with ICI as *the* model) thereby confining workers and their unions to a subordinated role outside of the management process.

It could be argued that, in Marxian phraseology, the material conditions for creativity and freedom are only now in place – potentially universally – through the communications revolution of new technology. The pessimists might retort that these, in commercial capitalist hands and with authoritarian power structures, may involve global media empires with new dimensions of manipulation, hierarchy and arbitrary power.

But insofar as principles of creativity and freedom are advanced, can they be given more definition? Can we clarify the individual or communal location of such human energy, or what the balance might be between freedom and responsibility?

We can hardly improve on principles suggested by Bertrand Russell (op. cit.), who argued:

1. *The growth and vitality of individuals and communities is to be promoted as far as possible.*
2. *The growth of one individual or one community is to be as little as possible at the expense of another.*[6]

In Russell's words, the second principle 'applied impersonally in politics' includes the principle of liberty as a part, but as applied by an individual in dealing with others 'is the principle of *reverence* [his emphasis] that the life of another has the same importance which we feel in our life'. We appear, then, to be back with the initial emphasis on one aspect of social solidarity. It should be added that for Russell 'community' is a very open category, not necessarily governmental and not necessarily geographical.

Understandably, the socialist tradition keeps returning to the principles that should apply to work. Here, certainly, the question of balance comes in. Not all work may itself be creative – though more could be designed to be so, and technology may relieve toil – but fairly shared work should not be onerous, and working hours should leave people a great deal of social space for creativity or freely chosen recreation and development. Democracy should extend to the work in industrial and service organisations and enterprises, not in an exclusive syndicalism of working producers, but in a shared process involving community concerns and the needs of consumers and users. To borrow again from Bertrand Russell, socialist concerns with creativity and freedom do not point to 'a static or final system'. If at this stage we attempt to identify the industrial democracy of the future we can sketch 'hardly more than a framework for energy and initiative'.

Notes to Chapter 4

1. 'Praxagora' – an interesting invented name on the part of Aristophanes; is this a version of consumerist socialism, skilled in the market place?
2. This is lovingly and painstakingly recorded in a vast array of British historical research from, *eg* Seebohm's *English Village Community* in the 1880s, Gomme in 1890, through to the C. S. Orwin's brilliant *The Open Fields* in 1938.
3. Quoted by R. W. Postgate: *Revolution* (1920).
4. Bertrand Russell: *Principles of Social Reconstruction* (London: Allen and Unwin Ltd, 1916).
5. Bertrand Russell: op. cit.

CHAPTER 5

Sources of Social Vision in the Christian Tradition

THIS chapter attempts to begin to speak of sources of social vision within the Christian tradition. It attempts to draw out some elements of the dynamic of that tradition as being creative for the task of responding to the present situation; for it is in that creative interaction of tradition and contemporary scene that a social vision may emerge, not in the imposition of a comprehensive formula from the past assumed to be valid *semper et ubique*.

The Bible itself is not a socialist manifesto, nor any other hue of manifesto. There are books in the Bible, such as Amos, which may come close to that, and certainly provide some appropriately ringing soundbites (albeit laced with some politically-incorrect references to the Cows of Bashan and suchlike). But to make of the Bible a coherent social programme requires a distortion which denies the variety of forms of literature contained in it, ignores the variety of socio-economic contexts to which different parts are addressed, and overestimates the internal consistency of meaning.

Certainly, there is a great deal of Biblical material dealing with the issues we have seen as ingredients of social vision. The liberation theologians' critique of western theology's techniques of evasion and spiritualising of the cutting edge of the Biblical demands for justice has ample justification (as any attempt to discuss such as the story of the rich young ruler with a typical congregational group might confirm). The pressure towards an interpretation which leaves the interpreter undisturbed is an insistent one, particularly when powerfully reinforced by the surrounding culture. But the reaction to that can often drift too readily toward a selective fundamentalism which demands that a range of texts be taken at 'face value' while others (such as those in the wisdom literature which equate riches with divine favour) are evaded or simply ignored.

With that serious reservation, however, it must also be recognised that there are valuable resources in the Bible for the building of a social vision, whatever view one takes of the authority of the Bible (or of later Christian tradition). There are clearly problems, however, with any excursion into public theology in a society very conscious of its pluralism. The standpoint taken here is that those who accept at some level the authority of the Bible as Word of God are at liberty (indeed under obligation) to offer the insights of that tradition to public debate, recognising that their position is not unique; when we speak we do so from our traditions, and that is not something for which we should be apologetic. What follows, then, is a far from comprehensive quarrying of the resources we may have to offer towards the building of social vision, from Biblical and later Christian tradition, recognising that this is not to claim any particular such vision as *the* Christian one.

Biblical Resources

The most obvious area for drawing on here is the prophetic books, with their scathing indictments of the comfortable rich and their outward piety. The persistent demand for social justice which rings through these books is clearly seen as the direct demand of God, evaded by the religious scrupulosity which attends to religious duties while neglecting the poor. That demand is addressed to rich and powerful individuals and to society at large, in the context of an 'embedded' economy which ultimately accepts divine authority, which in some sense seeks to reflect the divine nature in its social patterns. Our context, of a jealously guarded autonomy (if not superior authority) of economics, is – rightly or wrongly – quite different. Is the autonomous market of the 1990s immune from criticism or interference, or can it be re-embedded in a social vision which includes the demand for social justice (as the recent Commission on Social Justice struggled to do)?

Because the Old Testament tells the story of a people and their God, and because the divine demand for justice is addressed to the whole people, there is a substantial body of social legislation which recognises what poverty and inequality mean not only for individuals but for the whole community. In response to the divine demand for justice, a 'social security' system is built up which recognises the primary task of what we would recognise as state intervention through the legal and fiscal systems as being the protection of the vulnerable and the rescuing of those caught in downward spirals of hopelessness. The Sabbath and Jubilee years, for example, are designed in recognition of the fact that in markets the poor get poorer and the rich richer; intervention to renew hope by the possibility of a new beginning (in which, at regular periods, lands are restored to families who have had to sell or mortgage them, those sold into slavery are to be set free, and spiralling debts are cancelled) is needed to avoid the disintegration of society. Justice, then, is seen in terms of a recurrent need for a recalibration, for intervention that is not expected to secure equity for evermore but is needed to inhibit the injustice which builds on itself making lives increasingly impossible and undermining community. Such provisions also reflect the integration of faith and its festivals with social concern and the legislation which translates it into action.

The Old Testament history which is indeed the 'history of salvation' is the story of a developing social vision and the varying success of attempts to realise it; it is in the politics and economics of societies that God is working his purpose out. If the Exodus is the key, constitutive event in this history, it sets an ongoing agenda of liberation and concern for the oppressed which runs through such events in the story as David's gathering the oppressed and those who were in debt in the cave of Adullam. 'Remember that you were slaves in Egypt' runs the refrain which translates history into present demand for inclusiveness in society, from gleaning in the fields to holidays for the workers to invitations to the festivals.

These traditions are remarkably free from any glorification or spiritualising of poverty. Indeed, if the poor will, realistically, always be with us, that realism is not translated into complacent acceptance (by the powerful or the poor themselves); rather it demands constant attention. There is, then, a scepticism about the possibilities of a final justice in which poverty will be abolished, but a sense that rectifying justice is recurrently required. Poverty and hopelessness are to be tackled within a horizon of justice which is crucially different from the blindfold goddess with the balanced scales which characterises the western view. The Hebrew judge was more proactive than the Roman equivalent that has dominated our thinking, and the justice of the Old Testament (one of the horizons under which many of the threads of the story are held together) is not a coherent programme but a recurrent demand, always a concrete response to injustice rather than a formula which will degenerate into an idol.

If justice is transcendent, it can never be reduced to a programme, but continually demands new action. In the Old Testament (and beyond it), justice is relational, participative, dynamic/creative and partial. As relational, it focuses on relationships within the community, not to spiritualise these or freeze the patterns of a past generation, but to build the community which disintegrates under the pressure of unjust/unequal relationships. As participative, it refuses to accept exclusions from active membership in the community. As dynamic/creative, it does not pronounce after the event but acts to rectify injustice (and as such has forgiveness as a vital constituent). As partial, it recognises existing inequalities and therefore starts from a bias to the poor.

Hopelessness, and devices to undermine the possibilities of a new beginning, are therefore the antithesis of the justice which continually asserts that there is an alternative, and makes that assertion by struggling to build that alternative while recognising that that alternative itself will not be completely 'just'. The doctrine of original sin seems a helpful resource here, reinforcing a scepticism about final solutions and a recognition that 'the good that I would I do not', that good intentions do not guarantee the desired result.

The concept of covenant is another key to the understanding of the developing relationship between God and His people through the Old Testament and into the New. A covenant is more than just a solemn form of contract; covenant relationships reflect a more open-ended, deeper commitment to the relationship itself as crucial, in contrast to the limited instrumentality of contractual relationships which are the basic model for consumer society. Trust and forgiveness, which tend to be squeezed out by the contract culture, are vital elements of covenant. Equally, covenant relationships will take different forms in different times, whereas contractual relationships are defined by their own terms. They therefore embody conflicting concepts of justice; Hayek's limited justice has its roots in society understood as a network of contracts between individuals, where the deeper Biblical understanding sketched above takes shape within the covenant.

The hope and justice of the Old Testament are firmly located in this world as pragmatic concerns, but the interpretation of the New Testament has tended to remove both to a kingdom which is 'not of this world'. However, neither the divorce between spiritual and material nor the individualism that has dominated New Testament interpretation since the Reformation is necessary. The faith of those who gathered around Jesus was the faith largely of the Galilean poor, despised by the rich religious of Jerusalem;

when Jesus spoke of the poor and those in debt, his audience knew what he was talking about without translating it into a spiritual metaphor, and they located him in the prophetic tradition of protest and its bias to the poor. The vision becomes the kingdom of God, located beyond the present but a 'kingdom' nonetheless (*ie* a social vision not an individual one)[1], and the dimension of hope continues to look to the transformation of the world. Recent Biblical interpretation has also sought to rescue justice from the 'Reformation spectacles' that have determined its interpretation in Romans *etc*, restoring its social dimension as the relational, participative, dynamic, partial justice of the Old Testament, and opening the possibilities of forgiveness as liberating from the mistakes and oppressions of the past on the jubilee model.

Yet as Christianity spread through Asia minor, there are signs that it was no longer the faith of the poor. The primitive communism of Acts has been, and might still be, a powerful image of a Christian economic counter-culture; but in reality it was short-lived, probably tied into the expectation of an imminent end of all things and certainly did not translate into a radical political or economic agenda after the conversion of Constantine. Of course, the New Testament context (in contrast to the Old Testament) is of occupied Palestine where the economy was embedded in the culture of an alien Empire and any opportunity for disciples to have a say in the ordering of society was remote. In that context, the fact that the vision endured and was still the social one, of the kingdom, is perhaps more remarkable than any stress on the individual. Perhaps an equally important test of the Biblical social vision is to consider how it was translated into the thinking and practice of the churches.

Later Christian Tradition

The works of the Church Fathers can be quarried (and recently have been by Gonzalez) for material relevant to a social vision, though here again the churches have preferred to concentrate on their more 'religious' writings. But there is not a consistent socialist agenda here; to suggest otherwise is both anachronistic and highly selective. What is offered here is still selective (inevitably); the aim is not to summarise but to quarry useful resources for building a social vision for this country today.

For the first 15 centuries of the church, usury was a dominant (perhaps the dominant) concern of Christian ethics. This Biblical ban on interest (originally on all, not just exorbitant, interest) was a justice concern, that those who were poor and therefore in need of loans should not be exploited by those with the power to help them. It belonged to an age before commercial lending for capital projects, and even then faced severe 'market' pressures. A great weight of closely argued casuistry arose around it, and, crucially, it came to depend more on philosophical theories about the non-productive essence of money than on its original context of justice. Under the pressures of emergent capitalism and the Reformation, the shaky structure collapsed and now seems merely quaint, although Islamic banking operates, in principle, on an interest-free basis with some apparent success. Is it possible that a 'free' market in credit (one of many in which the poor pay more) might be challenged by justice concerns similar to those which fuelled the ban on usury? A small group – the Council on Monetary Justice – actively campaigns on this issue; if they are seen as marginal, they do at least represent an attempt to keep alive a major traditional concern.

The concept of sanctuary, rooted again in the Old Testament cities of refuge, also represents an important part of the practice of the church, sometimes in conflict with the state. It was not about the evasion of justice but about securing 'real' justice, and about the church as a place to which those with nowhere else to go could come. The way in which the debtors' sanctuary around Holyrood operated well into last century may not, with hindsight, seem so much a haven as a ghetto, but the need to offer hope to those in hopeless debt was recognised there. The churches of the US have recovered sanctuary in working with 'illegal' immigrants and it may well have other applications, particularly with those who are excluded from the consumer culture.

Similarly, the monastic movement may be seen as a protest against the loss of (social) vision. While there are dangers in a two-tier faith (the full rigour of the gospel for those in the Order but a different standard for those in the world, ironically parallel in a sense to Luther's two kingdoms), this can be (and was) seen as a counter-culture in which a social vision was being lived. Nor was it always divorced from the concerns of the outside world; it was the Franciscans who operated the *montes pietatis,* a kind of pawnshop in which loans for the poor at low interest were safe-guarded when the usury ban had failed to do so. On the other hand, many of the monasteries became rich and powerful players of the economic games of their time without offering a challenge to the game itself or the way it was played. Yet, within these limits, there is an authentic tradition of challenging social vision practised communally in the midst of society characterised often by voluntary poverty (as identification as well as religious virtue), by concern for equality and rejection of 'consumerist' values.

To what extent the Reformation may be seen as involving a social vision is a matter for debate. Certainly the radical (Anabaptist) wing of the Reformation found itself in alliance with radical political movements, but the mainstream came to be heavily dependent on the support of princes and other rulers and, lacking its own power-base, may be better represented by Luther's distancing of the reformers from the peasants' revolt. In Scotland, a similar dynamic may be seen in the alliance of the established Kirk with the power of the landowners inhibiting any substantial voice of resistance to the Clearances while the Free Church was able to resist that as well as patronage. The issue may be the extent to which the churches' social vision is limited by its predominant class constituency (of which more later).

The series of Papal 'social' encyclicals which stretches from *Rerum Novarum* (1891) to *Centesimus Annus* (1991) represents a developing tradition of social vision, which clearly varies in emphasis from the outright rejection of socialism to the stress on social justice which came to dominate Catholic and other church pronouncements in the 1970s and 1980s (with some retrenchment more recently). Some of the self-confidence of church statements on justice seems to have been undermined by current economic orthodoxy, although *Centesimus Annus* shares many socialist critiques of unfettered capitalism and indeed sounds in several passages more socialist than many of the pronouncements of the new Labour Party. There have been some consistent emphases – *eg* on the dignity of persons – and some particular insights – *eg* on subsidiarity – but variety in how these have been understood; the theme of the 'preferential option for the poor' had by the 1990s emerged into mainstream teaching from the liberation theology wing, and concepts like solidarity and justice for the oppressed were to be cherished rather than denounced as Marxist. There is clearly a considerable area of traditional common ground in the critique of capitalism in terms of what it does to people lacking the power of capital, and of what it does to authentic human relationships and values in society. There is an intertwining of Marxism and Christianity in *Centesimus Annus* which is not new but more clearly stated than before in light of the urgency of a dominant common threat. The alliance becomes much more fragile when it comes to advocacy of solutions or alternative models, but it will perhaps always be the church's role to offer both theological/theoretical and practical critique of the way things are, in the name of the life of the kingdom, challenging any current orthodoxy.

Equally important as the words has been the action, the social engagement of the Catholic churches. Though again this could not be claimed to be consistent, the worker priest movement (for example) may be seen as belonging here, and representing a determination that social vision be developed alongside the poor, by listening and pragmatic involvement.

In Britain too, the roots of the trade union movement, despite some opposition from the churches, can be seen as reflecting a strong Christian influence:

May you rejoice at all times in the lessening of human suffering, in the alleviation of human sorrow, and in the elevation of your fellowmen. Always let charity and wisdom guide you in your efforts, remembering that in aiding others in distress you are elevating yourself and that it is better to give than to receive

... so ran the initiation ceremony of the Boilermakers Union; and many of the early leaders of the movement (as of the Labour Party) – from the Tolpuddle Martyrs to Keir Hardie – were driven more by Christian conviction than by Marxism or any other secular world-view. Our own series of conversations in Easterhouse suggests that this basic Christian conviction (the 'loving your neighbour thing' as someone put it) is still more important as a motivation for community activists than any political ideology.

It would also be fair to recognise the prominent role of Christian conviction in the movements to abolish slavery, to improve prison conditions, to establish education for all, to build up 'social security', to resist nuclear weapons, and to boost overseas aid; each 'single issue' campaign represents substantially a bringing to bear of Christian social vision on particular injustices (without seeking to claim all the credit for the churches).

Historically, these seem far more important than either the Christian Socialist movement or the period of Christian Marxist dialogue in Europe. Certainly, that now-dated dialogue has exerted an important influence on the World Council of Churches and other ecumenical church pronouncements on social issues (although the real impact of such programmes as that on 'justice, peace and the integrity of creation' may not be great beyond the ecumenical circles in which they originate). The Christian Socialist movement does seem to be enjoying something of a revival in association with the leadership of 'New Labour', although some would question the appropriateness of 'socialist' as descriptive of the policies proposed.

Liberation theology offers crucial insights and challenges for the task of building social vision in this country; but it also has its limits. Its main challenge is to the extent to which academic theology attempts a false detachment from the culture in which it develops, and therefore the extent to which it evades Biblical demands, shares the assumptions of the privileged, and is complicit with the culture of contentment by justifying (or failing to challenge) the status quo. Its insights come from doing theology in a different way, namely in constant engagement with the lives of the poor, listening to what God is saying there and sharing in what God is doing there. But the crucial limits are precisely because of that; if we are to learn from liberation theology it is by our own engagement with what is happening in our own backyard not by importing a ready-made new theology or social vision.

One further chapter in the story is the surprising extent to which the churches played a crucial part in the resistance to Thatcherism. Christian social vision, built up during the previous two decades, continued to grow when other alternatives to the prevailing orthodoxy were in retreat. There is more here than the churches keeping alive last year's fashion; a tradition of values proved more resilient than most secular alternatives, and the churches' track record of ongoing work with the largely un-reported victims of the brave new markets earned a credibility for what was being said. The 'Sermon on the Mound' reflected Thatcherism's defensiveness here, and the greater strength of the resistance in Scotland (where also the Kirk retains a greater voice than the Church of England may now have); it also showed that Christian tradition can be plausibly mined for fuel for a very different social vision. Yet the Kirk, however critical the care-fully-argued work of the Church and Nation Committee may be, remains more Conservative (in its members voting habits) than the nation as a whole.

Tensions within the Tradition

Clearly the Christian tradition of social vision does not provide a consistent manifesto; like the socialist tradition it contains some ongoing tensions within itself, some of which are obvious from the above. Christianity may be said to be the most materialist of all religious, but the story of the church contains an enduring struggle between the spiritual and the material in terms of both practical and theological priorities; the tension between a theology which focusses on the individual's relationship with God and one which is more concerned with living out a faith in communities also runs as a thread through the story. For the churches themselves, there have been various historical ways of being 'in the world but not of the world', in the form of accommodations with state power in order to continue the 'religious' life of the church or challenges to that power, with accompanying persecutions; the relative ease of the churches present position in this regard in this country should not blind us to the pressures both now and then, both here and there. In the particular area of social vision, tensions can be clearly seen in Victorian Scotland between the Christian ideals from which the labour movement developed and the high Tory thinking and practice of someone like Thomas Chalmers (whose economic ideas have received high praise from supporters of the market revolution). And Biblically, there are distinctly different responses to wealth and poverty between the strain in wisdom literature which sees riches as a sign of divine favour (echoed loudly today in the American religious right) and the 'preferential option for the poor' (reflected in much of what has been cited above).

These tensions are intertwined, and it is not our purpose to isolate one strain as pure or authentic, but to draw on those elements which seem to offer most towards a Christian contribution to current debate. Perhaps the most significant Biblical tension here is between true and false hopes, but this is a different kind of tension from those just noted, in that it is a Biblical recognition of competing visions which quite explicitly defines some as authentic and others as destructive. Of course, the real tension lies in differentiating one from the other. True hopes, which do not disappoint us, are rooted in the experience of suffering. Hopes which disregard the realities of what theologians call original sin are false, but that need not commit us to policies which are based on, fuelled by and in turn themselves fuel individual greed.

Some Concluding Thoughts

The above is intended not as an attempt at a complete account, but as a catalogue of places where more detailed quarrying might inform our vision. It does establish a Christian tradition of social vision, against the criticisms of those who see it as the invention of a politicised clergy who

> *while increasingly losing their faith in a supernatural revelation, appear to have sought a refuge and consolation in a new 'social' religion, which substitutes a temporal for a celestial promise of justice, leading gullible folks into the dangerous error of making 'society' the 'new' deity to which we complain and clamour for redress if it does not fulfil the expectations it has created.* (Hayek)

To talk of a social vision at all, especially if it has justice as a crucial dimension, demands serious engagement with Hayek's critique (which is not attempted here). It also demands some wrestling with the sense that a vision which becomes a programme may become an idol; we cannot let the vision degenerate into identification with any set of policies, yet to be concrete it cannot run from commitment to particular pragmatic steps at particular stages along the way. What are the insights and experiences we can build on, and what dangers have we been alerted to?

Original Sin

Not immediately obvious as a building brick for vision, but when freed from the individualism and sexual focus of much Christian discussion this give a sense of realism to our social vision. The way in which one change can have unintended and unforeseen effects, the frustrations of intended good which fails to achieve its purpose, and a proper reluctance to identify any revolution or programme with the Kingdom or with the end of injustice are all important ingredients of a creative vision which aims to engage with the structures of sin which mean that 'good' people get involved in activities with 'bad' results regardless of their motives.

Forgiveness

In the Biblical context of justice sketched above, forgiveness is an inescapable part of the dynamic; it is part of how sinful structures are to be tackled. Again it may have to be disentangled from individualist understandings, but a social forgiveness which frees folk from the injustices of the past by facing them (not excusing or forgetting them) must be part of our vision.

Jubilee as Paradigm

The Biblical cluster of legislation for Sabbath and Jubilee years may never have been practised as they appear in Deuteronomy and Leviticus, yet they remain powerful images particularly as the millennium approaches – not as political programmes for today but as illustrations of what is necessary as interventions to prevent injustice building on injustice and denying hope. These laws tell of a recognition of growing inequalities as a recurrent fact of life, not accepted as 'the way things are' but demanding a corrective response. Justice here is seen as dynamic action to remedy injustices that will continue to appear.

Structured Generosity

The weight of Old Testament 'social justice' legislation, reinforcement in prophetic charges, and redefinition (but not privatisation) in parables like that of the labourers in the vineyard and in the practice of the early church, add up to a practical vision of a community in which care is neither left to the uncertainties of individual charity nor provided grudgingly by a state bureaucracy; that community may be said to be characterised by structured generosity.

Single Issue Campaigns

While the limits of such tackling of specific issues may seem to deny the broad sweep of vision we are seeking, none-the-less such represent perhaps the moments of most creative Christian leadership in this area (eg slavery, etc). Here alliances can be built, and objectives achieved which fuel hope. None heralds finally the kingdom, but, within the horizons of hope and justice that have emerged as the key characteristics of our vision, they represent real possibilities where vision can actually be enlarged rather than confined.

Hope

The orientation toward the future which originates in God's promise to Abraham, renewed to Moses and the people of Israel on the way to the promised land becomes eschatological in the New Testament. But Moltmann has shown that this is not to be a dismissal of concern for tomorrow; rather, hope is the key Christian resistance to any sense that there is no alternative, or that history has come to an end. Still, creation groans in childbirth as the new creation struggles to emerge painfully from the old.

Complicity and the Practice of the Churches

The social vision of the churches has been erratic and generally much more attuned to the spirit of the age (or the spirit of a particular group in that age) than we have recognised at the time; the churches' alliances and constituencies have limited its room for vision, most dangerously when we haven't realised what was happening. Our proclamation of a social vision has also often been undermined by the practice of the churches; can we speak about justice and equality in the world if the minister at Cramond is paid almost half as much again as his counterpart in Wester Hailes? Ultimately, however, we have a contribution we must make from the Christian tradition towards rebuilding a social vision; it must be in terms of justice and of hope, and it must find newly appropriate ways of expressing these on the way to the Kingdom. Part of that may take the (Biblical) form of parables which, like that of the labourers in the vineyard, may challenge accepted notions of justice while recognising that as the divine imperative.

Note to Chapter 5

1. Some liberation theologians prefer 'God's project' to 'God's kingdom'. Not only does that avoid the political connotations of kingdom, but it also emphasises God's ongoing engagement in the struggle for justice, as contrasted with an already-formed utopia.

CHAPTER 6

Christianity and Socialism: where Ways meet

In Conversation and in Common

WE have already indicated that we understand tradition not as a deposit from the past, external to us and unchangeable, but as a continuing and developing conversation in which our predecessors have engaged, we now engage and our successors will engage, and which involves both continuity and transformation.

We have just been describing what we consider to be important features of the two traditions, the socialist and the Christian, drawing particular attention to ways in which they have addressed matters of social vision.

For analytical purposes, we have treated them separately. This may have given the impression that they have been quite separate. This would be mistaken. The two circles of conversation, as it were, have sometimes overheard one another or more actively linked up with one another and even at times fused into a single circle of conversation; in other words, there has been interaction between the two traditions of varying degrees of intensity.

Our treatment of the two traditions separately has also shown a number of things which they have in common in their vision, theory and practice. However, it is in circumstances in which they have interacted, especially when the interaction has been deliberate, that what they have in common (and what not) and how they stand in relation to one another has become particularly clear.

Two rather different ways (not the only ones) in which interaction between the two traditions has taken place have been, on the one hand, when they have come together and sometimes even fused within the same people or group of people, and, on the other hand, when representatives of one or other or both of the traditions have deliberately instituted a conscious dialogue between them or an equally conscious examination by one of the other or by both of each other.

One example of the 'natural' fusion of the two traditions in the same people is often adduced, namely in British Methodism (cf Bernard Crick's view of British socialism as an 'eclectic fusion of Robert Owen's cooperative ideas, the cultural views of William Morris, Methodist conscience, Chartist democracy and revisionist Marxism'[1]). Another less well-known example is in some expressions of Scottish evangelicalism in the nineteenth century[2].

An example of the latter type of interaction, in this case a deliberate and conscious dialogue, was the Marxist-Christian dialogue of the 1960s associated with such writers as Roger Garaudy and Paul Oestreicher. More significant however is a very recent example of deliberate and conscious examination of one of these traditions by authoritative representatives of the other, namely the 1991 Papal Encyclical *Centesimus Annus*.

If traditions can be distinguished from one another as 'doctrinal' and 'non-doctrinal', or at least 'more doctrinal' and 'less doctrinal', with the doctrinal ones going beyond story, symbol and custom to self-conscious conceptualisation and systematic description, explanation and prescription, then both Christianity and socialism are doctrinal. We have been drawing attention to some of the important concepts in these two traditions. The affinities between these concepts are fairly evident. They are fairly explicit, so that there are words for them, the words which we have noted, like solidarity, forgiveness, justice, generosity, sin, hope and creativity.

However, doctrinal traditions contain also what might be called 'implicit doctrines'. They are not spoken, not because they are not important but because they are taken for granted; far from being less important, they are almost more important because they are foundational; the explicit doctrines are built upon them and presuppose them.

The close affinity between Christianity and socialism is borne out by the evidence that they share certain 'implicit doctrines', certain underlying and foundational assumptions about the nature of the human; one might say that they have common elements of philosophical anthropology. One could inquire into the source of these assumptions and ask whether they are *a priori* or *a posteriori,* whether derived from reason, experience, revelation or what, whether they are shared with other traditions than these two, whether perhaps the socialist tradition derived them from the Christian, and so on. We confine ourselves simply to drawing attention to these foundational assumptions. Two stand out, the second being a cluster of three-in-one.

Individuality and Sociality

The first shared implicit assumption is *the inseparability and mutual dependence of individuality and sociality.*
This assertion may surprise some readers. A form of individualism which cuts the cord between individuality and sociality and seeks to exalt the former and downgrade the latter has dominated much conventional wisdom in Europe and America in the last century and more; it has sought to demonise the socialist tradition as 'collectivist' and colonise the Christian tradition as sanctifier of its own individualism. But both these traditions, Christian and socialist, have assumed that human personhood is inescapably individual and social; that the concepts of individuality and sociality are incoherent without each other; that personal autonomy is dependent on interpersonal mutuality and vice versa; that being oneself and being with, for and in one another are inseparable. Both individualism and collectivism mistakenly assume a separability and foolishly seek to enhance one at the expense of the other; they lose themselves in abstractions that are far removed from reality. By contrast, for both the Christian tradition and the socialist tradition, selfhood and relationship with others are inseparable. For the Christian tradition this understanding of the human is closely related to its understanding of the divine and of the relationship between the divine and the human.

Resistant and Revolutionary Humanism

The second shared implicit assumption could be described as *a high view of human possibility.*
It leads on to two other stances – *an affront at much of human actuality* and *an assumption of the possibility and the necessity of transformation.*
The second assumption follows from the first, and the third follows from the combination of the first and the second. The first assumption, which governs the other two, could be sloganised as *humanism* and, adding the second and the third, it could be further sloganised as *resistant and revolutionary humanism.*
The first, the high view of human possibility, is central to the Christian tradition, being derived directly from the Christian understanding of the divine-human nexus; Christianity centring on the Christ as the epitome at once of the divine and of the

human, the fullest expression of both divinity and humanity. There could be no higher view of humanity, no higher humanism. Whereas much religion involves human reverence for the divine, at the heart of this religion is also a divine reverence for the human; Jesus is about God's belief in human beings as much as about human beings' belief in God. With this great reverence for human being goes a high aspiration for humanity, high hopes, a high view of its possibility. According to the Book of Genesis, human beings are in the image of God; according to the Psalmist, they are only a little lower than angels; and in case there should be any misunderstanding that Jesus is a human freak, an exception rather than the rule, he declares to his hearers that they will do greater things than he has done. It is clear that while the greatness has to do with what human beings already are, for they are revered as they are, it also has to do with what they can become, what they can come to be and to do; there is aspiration for them as well as reverence for them. Indeed their being is all bound up with becoming; one might almost say that the specially human thing is the blend of facticity with possibility.

It is also clear that the becoming is a matter of what they choose to become. Their own agency, their own decision, their own choice is involved. Their future greatness is not determined, fated, something that will simply be done to them; it is possibility not necessity; but it is possibility to be chosen by their decision, to be created by their agency; it is not the possibility of chance that will simply happen to them any more than the necessity of fate that will simply be done to them. It is something which they choose. The Deuteronomist says 'Choose Life' and the classic Christian evangelist declares 'Choose Ye This Day'. In this sense the future is open and to be chosen. Human being involves creating the future, choosing what to be and what to do.

The socialist tradition has a similarly high view of human possibility, and of human agency to actualise it. It belongs to a wider modern tradition, running through Renaissance, Enlightenment and their successors, which can be described as humanist. This modern humanist tradition has valued humanity highly, showing great respect if not reverence for human beings, entertaining high hopes for their future, and for the most part (with determinist exceptions) assuming that human agency is involved. Whether or not broad modern humanism is derived in part or in whole from the Christian tradition, the affinity is evident. Socialism is part of that tradition, with a particular emphasis on the sociality of the human which some more individualist elements of modern humanism have lacked (and which we have already discussed) and with an emphasis on the universality of the human which some more elitist elements of modern humanism have lacked. The most down-to-earth parts of the socialist movement have evinced with particularly great emotional power a profound reverence for all human beings, recognising that 'the man's the gowd for a' that', and a lofty aspiration for their future possibilities, believing that 'it's comin' yet for a' that'.

Second, alongside that high vision of human possibility there has been a great affront at much of human actuality. In that sense the humanism of both traditions is a resistant humanism, one that involves being affronted at what is and therefore protesting against it and countering it. It is a response to human actuality which is fired by the conviction of human possibility. It is that strange blend of sorrow and anger, which the minister in Lewis Grassic Gibbon's *A Scots Quair* calls the 'rage of pity'. It is evoked by all in the actual human condition which is a denial of reverence for humanity or aspiration for it.

In the prophetic strand of the biblical tradition, which is to be found in the canonical prophetic books and in Jesus, this angry sorrow or sorrowful anger is focused in poverty in the sense of the ways in which human beings oppress one another and diminish one another, the oppression being the face of poverty which denies reverence and the diminution its face which denies aspiration. In announcing and living out the 'regime of God', Jesus saw himself as herald and inaugurator of a counter-culture, his resistance to the existing order being based on his conviction of a possible alternative order.

It is true that this sorrowful and angry refusal to accept the actuality of human oppression and diminution is not present in the totality of Christian tradition. In periods when church and state have been in some form of alliance, there has been a readiness to accept the existing order. However, the dominant stance, in the tradition which Jesus in one sense inherited and in another sense initiated, is the prophetic affront which confronts. Sin in the sense of the flawed and distorted and distorting nature of the human situation and social order is understood by Jesus, and human beings are revered by him in spite of it; in that sense it is accepted by him. But it is confronted and resisted by him; it is not accepted in the sense that it is unchallenged or assumed to be unalterable. It is his later followers who have benefited from their contemporary social order who have changed the concept of sin from something to be seriously reckoned with in the process of transformation into something which rules out any transformation.

It needs little argument that such sorrowful and angry refusal to accept the actuality of human oppression and diminution is a feature of socialism. Its particular focus, at least in the modern era, is on the oppression and diminution associated with capitalist forms of social order. It too is an expression of an affront which confronts, protests, resists. So both traditions are forms of resistant humanism.

Third, both are also revolutionary, in the sense that they both assume the possibility and necessity of transformation. Because they believe in very high possibilities for humanity, they know that change from what is, is *possible*. Because they recognise that, by comparison with the height of human possibility, present human actuality is low, they know that change from what is, is *necessary*. Because the distance between the high possibility and the low actuality is so great, they know that the change which is both possible and necessary is root-and-branch or radical change, *ie* systemic change, with the thoroughness and comprehensiveness which that implies, in a word, transformation. The force of the term 'original' in 'original sin' is that the defectiveness is systemic, not that it is determining and impervious to change.

The Christian tradition in its New Testament expression is full of concepts and images of systemic change or transformation. The most general of these concepts is 'new creation'; there could be nothing more comprehensive and systemic than that. Other terms are new birth, new world or cosmos, new order or regime, turn round, whole mind change and, perhaps most potent of all, death and resurrection.

The socialist tradition may not have the range and depth of these big New Testament concepts of transformation, with their cosmic comprehensiveness and personal penetration. It may not speak of a new cosmos or of death-resurrection. But it is similarly concerned with systemic change and it does speak of new order and turn round. There may be disagreement between those Socialists who believe in sudden change and so are 'revolutionary' and those who believe in gradual change and so are 'reformist'; but whether the change be quick or slow, the end result is assumed to be 'revolutionary' in the primary sense of thoroughgoing transformation.

So both traditions are expressions of a humanism which is both resistant and revolutionary. Having a high view of human possibility and being affronted at much of human actuality, they regard transformation as both possible and necessary, and they pursue it.

Notes to Chapter 6

1. Crick Bernard: *In Defence of Politics.*
2. Mike McCabe: 'On Jordan's Banks: Some Thoughts on Evangelicalism and Socialist Revivalism in Scotland, in Andrew R. Morton (ed): *After Socialism? The Future of Radical Christianity* (Edinburgh: Centre for Theology and Public Issues, Occasional Paper No. 32, 1994).

PART THREE

From Present to Future: Forming Visions

INTRODUCTION

✳

IN Part One we addressed the experience of the loss of constructive social vision in contemporary Britain and we came to see
'hope' as a key concept. In Chapter 1 we suggested that hope, a
transformative vision of the future, is an essential ingredient to
proper social and personal life. The decline of public hope in Britain
over the past two decades was traced, as was the lack of hope of
two major groups in British society: the increasing number of the
dispossessed who, realistically, see little or no hope of greater participation in material and civic life; the contented who, paralysed by
fear of losing what they already have, dare not hope for a different
future. We suggested that a transformative hope can neither be a
future tense celebration of the (imagined) present nor a blueprint of
a definitive future but must be an ever unfolding horizon, guiding
us on a journey but not arriving at a final destination.

In Chapter 2 we considered the nature of religious hope – can
a transformative hope in our cold and materialist times be founded on religious, specifically Christian, grounds? In particular we
discussed the difficulty of acting in 'the middle', acting in the
insecure space between celebrating the present as the only possible society (yet another 'end of history') and withdrawing from
a rejected present into an uncontaminated enclave of the right-
eous. In the Crucifixion there is presented an image of the necessary risk of love, this acting in the middle, the unconditional but
rational offering to the other with no guarantee even of audience.
Tenable hope for a more just society must, we maintained, contain
this element of losing self (interest) in order to gain self: we gave
to this vision the term 'structured generosity'.

In Chapter 3 we addressed the two major visions of post-war
Britain suggesting that, in their combinations of the personal,
collective, moral and material, these gave us grounds for dis-
tinguishing between false and authentic elements in hope.
Thatcherism, the proximate cause of the contemporary loss of hope,
offered a false hope in seeing a certain version of contemporary

Western societies as the realisation of the universal in which the material becomes the moral and the personal, while the collective is reduced to the largely oppressive apparatuses of centralised state control. We suggested that securing the (temporary) complicity of ordinary people was the key to Thatcherism, especially through the sale, specially discounted for existing owners, of vast tracts of social capital. These privatisations contained within them the seeds of their re-socialisation in the form of extensive mechanisms regulating monopoly capital in the name of consumer interests in areas of basic need.

In Part Two we discussed the nature of two traditions which, historically, have been the source of transformative vision in Britain, Christianity and socialism. Are these traditions exhausted or can they contribute to a vision of a society of 'structured generosity'? In Chapter 4 we argued that ideas of common property and common rights can be traced in Western culture from at least the fifth century BC. Some of the tensions within this tradition, between utopian and Marxist, and between syndicalist and central state versions of socialism, were specified. This variety of the socialist tradition was, we suggested, held together by three core values: the requirements of social solidarity; the search for social justice; the emphasis on personal and collective creativity and freedom.

Similarly, in Chapter 5 we quarried the Christian tradition, particularly the Old Testament tradition, for elements of social vision. The vision of justice as relational, participative, creative and restorative found in these sources is combined with a scepticism about arriving at any final, just state. Here justice is a never ending process of rectifying the injustices, and forgiving delicts, which spring up despite even the best intentions. The concept of covenant, an ongoing, open-ended commitment to a relationship was contrasted with the narrow notion of contract. More recent contributions from the Christian tradition, to thinking about debt, to the abolition of slavery, to the birth of trade unionism, to liberation theology and, importantly, to Scottish resistance to Thatcherism, were also surveyed, not as an unambiguous legacy from Christianity to socialism but as contributions to a social vision of structured generosity. In Chapter 6 we suggested that the two traditions share four core assumptions: the mutual dependence of individuality and sociality; a high view of human possibility; affront at human actuality; and a belief in both the possibility and the necessity of human transformation.

In Part Three, on the basis of our considerations in Parts One and Two, we turn to the problem of how visions of society characterised by structured generosity might be formed. In Chapter 7 we consider the dialectic between the seemingly opposed notions of love, with all its overtones of arbitrariness and irrationality, and law, based on rationality and impersonal systems. We suggest that this is a false opposition, with detrimental consequences, and that law and love are necessarily inscribed in each other as ongoing processes. In Chapters 8 and 9 we explore two outstanding features of the present context for developing visions of a society based on the marriage of love and law, and of generosity and structure. The first, which we treat in Chapter 8, is the 'mixed economy' which combines market and welfare, private and public sector. The second, which is treated in Chapter 9, is the development of 'civil society' leading to the development and interaction of three sectors, public, private *and* voluntary.

Finally, in Chapter 10 we attempt to draw together the threads of our argument, not in order to produce our own particular vision, but in order to suggest 'materials and methods' for the task of vision formation in which as many citizens as possible should participate. This is in three parts, 'Some Hints', 'Some Theses' and 'Some Glimpses', the last consisting of brief accounts of six developments which we consider to be illuminating pointers to the future.

CHAPTER 7

Law and Love

WE argued previously that we need vision to give us the love to make the jump that would be both personally and socially transformative. That vision would also give that act of love rational underpinning. It would make the act of love something more than the empty quixotic gesture best characterised by the slogan 'All you need is Love'. Here we explain how one cannot separate love from law; how they are not mutually opposed but that the latter is implicated in the former; how the arbitrary explosion of love carries within it the seeds and bonds of rationality. This is what we mean by structured generosity, and more specifically, it is how what appear to be the anti-nomian values implicit in welfare mesh with the nomian values found in the law and the market.

Law and Love in the Good Samaritan

We begin our explanation with the parable of the Good Samaritan. That story starts off with a lawyer asking Jesus what he should do to gain eternal life. Jesus gives an answer in terms of the Law – 'Love God and thy Neighbour as thyself.' The context of this parable is that Jesus is seen as consorting with those who stand outside the law and thus putting himself outside the law. It will not do to say that this is precisely what is intended and that Christ came to overturn the law. Neither does it mean the opposite. Jesus came to 'fulfil the law', but that does not mean that the arbitrariness of love or welfare is left out. Were that the case, it would mean treating the legal way of looking at it as solving the question; that all that is needed is a definition of neighbour which can be applied without question. This way of looking at it, by exclusionary definition, can be seen applied in present day law. Thus Lord Atkin said in Donoghue *versus* Stevenson:

The rule that you are to love your neighbour becomes in law: You must not injure your neighbour, and the lawyer's question: Who is my neighbour? receives a restricted reply. You must take reasonable care to avoid acts or omissions which you can reasonably foresee would be likely to injure your neighbour. Who then, in law, is my neighbour? The answer seems to me to be persons who are so closely and directly affected by my act that I ought reasonably to have them in contemplation as being so affected when I am directing my mind to the acts or omissions which are called in question.

What the parable is doing is not laying down a definition of neighbour but saying that that person is your neighbour to whom you act in a neighbourly manner. You constitute the relation of neighbourliness by your actions. The parable says that neighbourliness is something that you do rather than something that exists. But surely this begs the question? You still have to know whom it is that you have to be neighbourly to before you can constitute the neighbour relation by your act. But this would be to separate elements which are, in reality, two sides of the same coin.

To make this clearer, let us take some recent cosmological theories. On a version of the 'big bang' theory of the universe, one might say that the universe starts from the explosion of a singularity. That explosion is arbitrary; there is no reason for it and yet that explosion carries within, in its unfolding, rationality in the shape of time and scientific laws. We can only make sense of causality, for example, because the big bang, in its explosion, unfolds time. Scientific rationality might stem from an arbitrary act, the explosion, but that does not make it irrational, for the rational is inscribed in the arbitrary and *vice versa*. To return to the Samaritan then: it would be a mistake to think of the act of the Samaritan as simply an arbitrary act of love which he does and then walks away from. For that act of love/welfare carries its rationality, in the shape of the bonds of obligation inscribed within it.

Take a more prosaic example. People ask if they can stay with you to visit the Edinburgh Festival. You offer them hospitality and invite them to stay and use your home as a base. If this is not too pretentious, you have given out of your love something that they need. But that, as we know only too well, is not the end of it. For your guests then ask if they can take you out to dinner, and though you might not want to go, your obligation as host makes you do that. But it does not stop there. Because you know the town, and they do not, then you have to find a restaurant which will be appropriate, in the right price range *etc.* So the first act of love (there was no particular reason why you should let *them* stay in your house) carries inscribed within it the bonds and the rationality of the host relation. The law is already inscribed in the act of generosity and one cannot escape it. A useful, though not full, analogy would be the rescue cases in English and Scottish Law. Roughly, though there is no duty to rescue, once someone starts trying to help another the law relating to negligence applies. The arbitrary act of rescue comes within the realms of the law; it has the law inscribed within it and one cannot get away from it.

So Jesus was not saying that the law does not matter; on the contrary, he was saying that to gain eternal life one must follow the law. But to follow the law is not merely a matter of understanding it. That is why Jesus answered the lawyer who was trying to catch him out in the way that he did. One applies the rule because it is right, but the rule can't itself make this the right thing to do. Yet the application, as a mysterious explosion of love, carries within it the bonds of rules and rationality. The Good Samaritan applies the rule 'love thy neighbour' to someone who only becomes a neighbour in that application, and thus by that loving act comes within the purview of rules and rationality. And so, though Jesus 'feasted with publicans and sinners', he did not put himself outwith the law, treating it as a matter of no consequence. The loving act was part of the lawful act.

It would be a mistake to think of this as all there is to the parable of the Good Samaritan and we will return to it later. At the moment the point is to say that love and law are aspects of each other and cannot be separated. There is no law without love, there is no love without law. Neglect of that fact contributes to a false and distorting polarisation of law and love; a polarisation which leads on the one hand to the soulless force of formal rationality and, on the other, to the always frustrated search of immediacy .

The reason we have put the dichotomy in this way is that ironically both the left and the right, at the extremes, agree with the thesis that market society and law, in the sense that we have been talking about, are inextricably linked. And so the dichotomy on both sides is that market and welfare, which is seen as an anti-market principle, cannot be conjoined. It is a zero sum game, having one implies the absence of the other. Thus the market is said to drive out welfare and love in our society, and in a welfarist society, welfare is said to drive out law and legality.

Law and Love among the Labourers in the Vineyard

To explain this more fully, we turn to the parable of the Labourers in the Vineyard. Here, it appears that God's love comes up against the demands of the labourers to be treated equally. The master gives to each what they need for a day's subsistence. Out of his love he gives them what they need and this captures the sort of arbitrariness that love/welfare has. One way of reading this parable is as saying that love has no reason, that the particularity of love is something that trumps equality, that the cry for the application of equality and the rules by the labourers is as nothing against the love of God. But to look at it merely as a way of saying that love trumps the demand for the rationality of bonds and obligations would be a mistake. For the act does create bonds and thus rationality. The master says: 'Friend, I do thee no wrong: didst not thou agree with me for a penny? Take *that* thine *is*, and go thy way: I will give unto this last, even as unto thee. Is it not lawful for me to do what I will with mine own?'

We should not read it the other, pro-market, way, as stating the obvious truism that contractual acts create obligation. What is important about the act is that it is appropriate in the first place, 'Is thine eye evil, because I am good?' It is lawful 'to do what I will with mine own', but only because 'I am good'. It is the goodness of the act that unfolds into a system of obligations. We might argue that the parable is rigged since it is God who is the master. He is a special case, being all knowing as well as all good. Since God knows all, he knows what is best for everyone; being all good, he can be trusted to will it for everyone; by being all powerful, he can achieve it for everyone. However, we cannot be God and so cannot know the best thing to do.

This can be taken as the nub of an argument for the market and against welfare and state intervention. God might know what every individual human being is doing and what is best for him or her in the context of what everyone else is doing, but this is beyond the capacity of human beings. Caring only works if you know what you are doing. This is an argument for a sort of defensive strategy. An over-arching system of rules implying equal treatment under equal general rules is the only rational way that human beings can live in community. It may be unnatural but that is all to the good for it is a step above our primitive emotions and need for security. It is a move from the morality of the tribe, the solidarity of the small group, to the good society where everyone is united through general rules. We may not have the depth of feeling in such a society but that is the price we pay for our civilisation. In the same way the market is the way in which we can rationally organise ourselves in the conditions of not being able to know everything.

This conflict between what people still feel to be natural emotions and the discipline of rules required for the preservation of the open society is indeed one of the chief causes of what has been called the 'the fragility of liberty': a community, by directing the individuals towards common visible purposes, must produce all attempts to model the Good Society on the image of the familiar small group, or to turn it into totalitarian society.[1]

But this would be a wrong tack to take. For one of the things about the teaching of the parables is that you do not know the answer. The great parable of the judgement where everyone is divided into sheep and goats is awesome and terrifying precisely because everyone is surprised, neither set of people know why and for what reason they are saved or not. The imagery of losing one's life in saving it is shown clearly in the parable of the talents. Our life is a risk and in refusing to accept that risk by acting out of love is the surest way of destroying it.

But the argument is more than defensive. The system is one where individual actings are co-ordinated through markets not merely because this is what markets were designed for but because markets turn out to have this property. They do so because in an open market there is a tendency for activities to be co-ordinated. Those are rewarded who produce a commodity that is desired at the lowest price. The market is the most efficient system of communicating the information, in the form of prices *etc*, that people need to achieve that goal. In the pursuit of their own interest, they are led to favour the general interest. The metaphor that best describes this is that of the 'invisible hand' According to Raphael this is not meant to be taken as a theological metaphor in its original use by Adam Smith. In one sense this is true and we are not to understand this as though there is some presence, divine or otherwise, guiding everything so that the incommensurable desires of all end up in a rational and co-ordinated plan. Rather, what we have is a system where the intentional actions of many particular people can be co-ordinated and made coherent. This can be effected without these people having to desire the particular outcomes that the system as a whole brings about. Thus an absence would be a more appropriate way of talking about it.

However we can also see this as a product of the theology of the time, stemming from Newton's theology and from his idea of the universe as a machine with all pieces fitting together. The function of God, being not to keep it in motion but rather to oil it occasionally. So the market system is designed as a self contained rational system of co-ordination. In Thomas Chalmers this also played an important part in his theodicy in that God had so arranged the world that the selfish impulses of people were functional in providing rational social order. So the God of the oil-can also becomes the God of the night watchman state. In a world designed like this one does not need intervention, except the occasional oiling. Indeed active intervention would be positively harmful. The parable challenges that sort of story for it shows an interventionist God.

But that does not thereby show the falsity of the market story. For it is in the act of love that knows no reason that the rational order comes into being and is sustained. Put less parabolically, liberal societies like ours, which rely on the close intertwining of the rule of law and of the market, can only be kept going by institutions which are not of that kind. The market and legality are not self generating and depend upon institutions which are not like them. They depend on acts of love and generosity. The trust and love necessary to keep the system going cannot be generated internally since this is precisely what the market eschews. It is however a dialectical process. To use the imagery that we started off with: we need the big bang and that big, arbitrary explosion is the obverse of the system rationality which both needs it and is sustained by it and, lest we want to throw system rationality away altogether, is sustained by that very rationality. To return to cosmological theory again, to explain the beginnings of the universe is not just a matter of explaining how a string of black paint came to be on an empty white canvas. We have to explain how the canvas and frame came to be there as well. And one explanation of that would be that the explosion of black paint creates the frame and canvas which then also creates and determines the paint. But for society a one off explosion is not enough. The society can only be sustained by a continuous explosion of acts of love which both sustain that society and determine the acts of love. A steady state big bang theory of creation then, is the best way of explaining what we have in mind.

The Relation of the Morals of the Market and the Morals of Welfare

Unless we see this dialectical relation, all we see is as a collection of moral pluses and minuses on each side with no way out. How do we conclude then? If we go to the Labourers in the Vineyard we seem to be on the side of everyone at once. We see that the disappointed labourers have a point and we also approve of the love shown by the master. Is this an example of our wanting to have our cake and eating it? Only if we consider that the two principles are contradictory and that one must drive out the other. This is in fact how many have considered it. What we now turn to is to show what it is the market gives, in its moral minus, and how that is converted to a moral plus with the addition of the love that knows no reason, and how in turn that love in its moral minus is converted to a moral plus with the addition of the rationality of the law.

The market with its emphasis on rationality and the law seems to act in such a way where, contrary to Hayek, we seek the easy way. By following the iron laws of the market or the law, we avoid the peril and danger of setting aside these laws and putting ourselves in the unknown. Though the market might provide enterpreneurship and dynamism in social life, it also morally seeks to evade responsibility; the consequences do not matter as long as I follow the rules and the iron laws of my preferences. In that way we seek the moral comfort zone. We do not risk because we do not want failure and there is no failure in the market because all outcomes are acceptable as long as the rules are followed. That breeds a legalistic morality. It concentrates on the rules to the exclusion of everything else, the rules lose their sense of con-tingency. They dominate the entire moral universe. They are the islands of stability in a chaotic universe. This concentration on law and the rules makes us forget that it is we who make the rules and we that can change them. We see ourselves instead as the techni-cians of rules that we do not and cannot challenge. The morality of law becomes one of legalism; of the technical rational manipu-lation of rules. The rules have a life of their own which cannot be challenged. They control us rather than we control them. What we concentrate on is the rules themselves. We follow them and do not think about what they say. And of course we think ourselves justified. This is well illustrated by the Pharisee as he stands in the temple proud that he obeys the laws and is not like the sinners. Jesus damns that Pharisee.

We can see the moral effect of this through another example. Think of the automated systems for drawing money out of one's bank account. You put your card in the machine and key in your Personal Identification Number (PIN). If you are in credit and various conditions have been fulfilled, then you get your money. But if you have no money or have already taken out your quota for the day, no cash is issued and there is no arguing. The machine does not see you, the person who might need the money there and then for all sorts of pressing and important reasons. The machine is not interested in you it only 'sees' the card. It sees (reads) that and it says that no money is to be given to you. What you think or what you can say is unimportant. You have now become the card. You no longer exist for the bank and it is only your card that exists. We have used the example of the machine to make the example more graphic. The machine could be the social security clerk as he or she applies the regulations, you as you follow the law.

It is in this way that love is negated by rules. For love and fellow feeling cannot get in the way of the operation of the rules. But of course, there is a plus side to all of this which we see if we take the perspective of the labourers in the parable of the Labourers in the Vineyard. Here the rationality of rules is all important. Think of the cash machine analogy again. Say the machine becomes a teller who cares. They do not see you as the cash card. Rather they see you as someone in need. Their love goes out to you and they give you money. But if they keep doing this, listening to their feeling, then where will all the money come from? Will the bank have any left? What about the depositors? For the sake of helping a few they might have harmed the many. It is the rules and the machine-like activity of the law that keeps that in check. What one needs is a way of knowing when to stop acting like the machine and not follow the set patterns, when to let the person in the card break out. Or, to put it more pro-saically, when creatively to break or re-think the law. Or to put it in market terms, when do we need non-market principles?

The Morals of the Market and the Morals of Welfare in Institutional Practice

We now turn to some of the effect of these points in institutional practice. Let us look more closely at the law and the trial. What are the implications of some of the points which we have been making? Within the trial, we might say that this process makes the defender invisible. What does this mean? G. K. Chesterton (1960) in his detective stories makes this clear. In one he gives us the classic locked room mystery. Someone is murdered in a locked room, the sole entrance to which has been kept under observation. No one was seen. Who did it? The answer is the postman because no one noticed him. Since he was always there he was invisible. Think of the way some people have treated, and treat, their servants. They are people who perform certain functions and who never get in the way – never appear to be there. People would say that they were alone when in fact surrounded by servants. Indeed this ability to treat the servant as invisible was seen as a mark of the upper class.[2] The trial process is analogous. The defender in the trial is not the concrete human of the concrete world. He is, as described above, a legal person, the abstract bearer of rights and duties. This means that nothing is relevant in the trial except those things which are relevant to proving liability. Political, moral and social opinions, particular concrete circumstances that the person finds themselves in are excluded. He has no history because the only thing that is at stake is liability in respect of the rules. The things that he might see as important are often ruled as irrelevant because they do not determine liability. That is all that is at stake. The trial becomes what Garfinkel[3] calls a degradation ceremony. What this does is strip real persons of all their concrete humanity so that they become literally invisible, unnoticed and irrelevant. The classic examples of this are in 'closed institutions' such as mental homes. There the inmates might just as well not exist though they are the *raison d'être* of the institution. Some research in the courtroom has been struck by the almost literal irrelevance of the defender. The trial could go on just as well without him or her.

The above is one way of describing the trial process. But another way would be to say that this invisibility protects the defender. Because it prevents prejudice as to the particular sort of person they are from determining the result. The defender is not subjected to a humiliating trial where all aspects of their life and history are looked at and exposed to public view. Indeed, if we look at rape trials, the complaint has been that there is not enough of this indifference which above was seen as morally questionable. Here the moral question is whether an innocent women's sexual history should be paraded before the world and all sorts of erroneous inferences made from it. The trial process is aimed at preventing that from happening. And that is the down side of caring. In the trial context caring can too often degenerate into a journey to the inmost soul of those involved.

Let us now turn to health provision. In *The Gift Relation* Titmuss[4] compares the free donation of blood with the selling of blood and what consequences it has for welfare. For him the turning of blood into a commodity means that nothing is sacred and that

> ... *all policy would become in the end economic policy, and the only values that would count are those that are measured in terms of money and pursued in the dialectic of hedonism. Each individual would act egoistically for the good of all by selling his blood.*

The implications of this are that the relation between doctor and patient would change if the system of heath care was market-based. Treating someone as a customer rather than a patient will have certain consequences. The relation changes from 'caring' to 'providing services for a client'. 'Defensive medicine' is more prevalent in a market system. Here, treatment is not merely dependent on the doctor's judgement of need but also in order to avoid law suits in the future. Litigation is much more common in America than it is here. Medicine is pushed into areas where money will be made rather than where there is real need. Cosmetic surgery becomes more important. The relationship of trust disappears to be replaced by the wary relationship of the man of business.

Should the health service be like that? We might think not, but are we not being naive when we think that in the non-market system we will always be able to trust doctors. Here, all the problems of professional power are raised again. We must bear in mind the fears, raised by Hayek and others, that we discussed earlier. What will happen in a society where those who think they know best dictate to others? True, the actual structure of the relationship will change. But is that necessarily bad?

One final example. Lawyers are often held to make the painful process of separation worse. One reason for this is that they will practise 'defensive lawyering'. The parties might come to an informal and amicable arrangement where one gets less than they are legally entitled to. Defensive lawyering means they will be advised of the full extent of their rights. This might create suspicion and tension. It might produce a fight where before there was agreement. Is this bad? We might not want to make divorce harder. But how do we know that the informal arrangement is truly acceptable if both sides do not know their real rights? In the long run, it might make matters worse.

In the former societies of Eastern Europe, non-market principles were applied everywhere, including economy and law. In the West, there was, and indeed still is, an attempt to marketise all fields of social life, including the 'caring' institutions. For the Marxists, the commodity form (the market principle) tended to spread and infect all forms of social life. For the liberals, command economy principles tended to spread and drive out the other forms. This might be true as a matter of sociological and historical fact. Powerful institutions in society do spread their values and their ways of going about things. This is not necessarily the case. Society is not a site of logically contradictory or counter principles where the one drives out and hides the other. To the contrary, social life and its institutions are a based upon a mixture of principles which are in tension, one with the other. Particular social institutions will resolve this tension in different ways. They will balance the principles in particular ways in differing concrete circumstances. But this will not be a compromise in the sense that more of one will mean less of the other. The point is that this will not be a compromise in the sense that having more welfare means less legality etc. When we come to looking at political institutions we will not necessarily justify them by the grand and abstract principles of 'freedom' or 'welfare'. Thus the market definition of absence of coercion will not be the one always applied. Freedom from poverty, freedom to organise, etc will also be in play. These particular freedoms will be pursued at particular times and places and will be weighed against each other. Likewise with welfare, this will mean different things in differing circumstances and differing concepts will be balanced against each other. State intervention in declining areas no more breaches the market principle than do aspects of the market in heath and education. The problems of choice that arise in political life will not be susceptible to reduction to one principle or another.

When we look at institutions in our society then the question is not the abstract one of whether market or welfare principles are best. We cannot rule out market or welfare principles *per se*. The solution to problems of professional power will depend on the particular circumstances involved. Solving them by marketisation or 'customer power' will not be appropriate in all cases. Compare students, patients, passengers and prisoners. Should all the areas involved, education, health, transport and the prison system, have customers instead? Do market principles for the distribution of goods necessarily detract from the principle of care? Is it the same in health and education (cf Le Grand and Estrin, 1989; Dworkin, 1985; Raz, 1986)?

Legality will not prevent child abuse, but it might prevent social workers abusing the rights of children and their parents. Legality and the welfare principle are both necessary. Legality is not compromised by the introduction of lay justice and welfare principles, rather the institutions of social regulation are thereby made stronger.[5] Both are necessary.

Markets, Love and Community

We finally turn to the interconnections between the market and love and what that means for community. Part of the problem is that those who follow Hayek forget that at some level it is justified in terms of outcome. The market is justified as the best way of acting for the general interest. But what if, as is clear in some cases, it does not? The trickle down effect is supposed to make everyone well off but it has not. It seems illogical to say we cannot intervene because we do not know individual preferences but at the same time, when we know general outcomes, and they are not what we claimed the system would generate, to refuse to intervene. If the justification for doing nothing is because we cannot know, then when we do know we should do something.

The problem is that in some respects the internal workings of the market, that way of getting rational outcomes through individual selfishness, carries over to the reason we might have had the market in the first place, that is to produce a sort of collective love (contrary to some of the social contract and possessive individualistic stories). We can see studies that show how the market production of the notion of equality enables us to produce intimacy and friendship that is no longer dependent on power relations. Thus we can now be enjoined to love not merely through helping the poor. And we can produce the collective security that enables us to deal with poverty and we do not need it to practice our love. In recent times Scandinavian systems, especially the Swedish ones, have been leading examples of that.

Now this might appear to be an attack on the image of the parable of the Good Samaritan with which we started. For that seems to depend upon a pre-modern conception of community where people needed love because they were poor and thus were dependent and vulnerable. 'Give us this day our daily bread' is now, in the West at least, replaced by love and intimacy which are based on equality and respect. And this enables us to have general love in abolishing the poor and creating collective security which partly comes through the manipulation of the market. So we do not need the poor in order to save ourselves by practising that kind of charity. But it would be a mistake to think of the parable as enjoining us to practice charity through helping the poor.

First of all, that does not appear to be what the parable is actually saying. The parable is in answer to the question 'who is my neighbour' – it is understood that the law 'Love thy Neighbour' is to be obeyed. And the neighbour in the story is the Samaritan. So the person we are enjoined to love is not the 'the man fallen among thieves' but the Samaritan who helps him. It appears then that it is not the poor we are to love but the rich! What can this mean? This is not part of the master slave dialectic nor are the poor being asked to love those who help them because they help them. It is a much deeper and more profound relationship than that. As we saw, the answer Jesus gives in the parable is impeccably within the law. But he is not thereby privileging it. The question implicitly put by the lawyer is turned on its head. His question is to whom should I extend the comfort and safety and privilege that I have in the law. Jesus changes it to something like; 'to whom should one turn when in the direst need, thereby extending the hand of brotherhood and community?' And the answer that Jesus gives is shocking and challenging. For he says that in that case you entrust yourself to your worst enemy. But it is even more than that. He is not saying this to the 'man fallen among thieves' rather he is asking the lawyer to consider it. So he is asking the lawyer to think of himself in need and dependent and to seek from those whose response might be unwelcome and unexpected. And what that is saying is that we should consider community not as a group of autonomous self sufficient individuals but as people who are vulnerable and need each other. And even if we consider ourselves autonomous and self-sufficient, we are to consider ourselves in need. That vulnerability is something that is beautiful, something that makes humans what they are. This is something that the Greeks saw, when they thought of the fragility of human goodness as something that in its bitterness was beautiful, and what the God who sends his only Son to die on the cross acts on.

So the supporters of workfare which aims to attack 'the dependency culture' do not want to risk disruption to their comfortable world. They will minimise the risk of that disruption and the problems of giving to those whose reception of the gift might be unexpected and unwelcome by constructing those worthy of the gift in their own image. That image is one of self sufficiency and autonomy. Hence to receive you must work. The act of giving is also the act of receiving and they do not want to receive the gift of vulnerability. On the other hand, those who receive might also find it irksome because they have to accept that they are part of community with those who seem to oppress them and, moreover, they have to accept that they are vulnerable as well. In this context it is important to note that the man who was helped was a Jew and thus within the law. What that means then is that we are asked to consider that being within the law is not somewhere where one can be proud in one's safety and security. It is a vulnerable place which needs acts of love (the Good Samaritan) to sustain it and that act receives the gift of the vulnerable law. Giving and receiving are interconnected because they are about sharing vulnerability and love.

Why is all this apposite to the Swedish case? Part of the Swedish system in relating benefits to work gives everyone an incentive to stay in state systems of insurance and not opt for private ones. So giving benefits to all in work or not and not just targeting them to the needy means that there is an incentive to keep these benefits and the state care systems that they engender. Thus collective security enables poverty to be dealt with. Targeting to the 'needy' gives those who have the money and influence no incentive to fight for state benefits and therefore they tend to be lower in those systems. But part of the dynamic of that is that people care less for others because they are cared for collectively and Sweden is characterised by even more distant personal social relations than those found in the more market oriented countries. In the latter, people know the market engenders distant social relations; they care randomly to cope but do not locate that as in anyway linked with the market rationality. In the former, people think that the system of market interventionist rationality collectively cares so they care even less themselves because, ironically, the system rationality does it for them. But where that might lead to in the end is the end of the system of collective care because it has lost the individual explosions of love that keep it in being. People do not care because they care collectively but they only care collectively because they care individually and so we have a vicious circle. It is no longer a steady state big bang system. The explosions of love which are needed to keep re-inventing the rationality of the system in general are missing. In organising in terms of the system rationality of self preference we loose the need for them. This is not to say that we need to get rid of the principle of universality in these cases. Rather it is that the principle needs to be re-invigorated constantly. We need to make sure that opportunities for the explosions of love that keep it going are always there.

The answer to this can be seen in one way of understanding the linking of the personal and the political, individual love with collective security. Two images from the Gospels help here. The first, the judgement scene in the Gospel of St Matthew and the other, Christ on the Cross. St Matthew says:

> *Then shall the king say to them that shall be on his right hand: come ye blessed of my Father, possess you the kingdom prepared for you from the foundation of the world.*
>
> *For I was hungry, and you gave me to eat; I was thirsty and you gave me to drink; I was a stranger and you took me in.*

(25: 34-35)

The majesty and importance of this passage is that it is God who is here encountered and helped. A God, not almighty and omniscient, but poor and thirsty; vulnerable in the sight of His creation.

The second image is that of Jesus on the Cross, suffering the concrete, human, and particular pains of the crucifixion. At the same time that figure on the Cross is the embodiment of all-encompassing reason, of the principle of reason and rationality that we name as God.

These two images show something about the personal in politics. They show how the particular individual must never be lost in everlasting rationality. The profundity is that it is not just something like saying that what you do in your individual life is a reflection also of your general politics. It is about how you *encounter* the general. How what you do in those situations is your general politics. Our system rationality is tested in the crucible of that encounter. In that encounter, we recognise, as did the Good Samaritan, the divine vulnerability, the beauty and need in all others and ourselves. But though the love is unconditional, it does not mean that it is weak and omni-tolerant. What we have in mind here is a hard love, not a situation where 'everything goes'. Love is about learning as well. We accept those in need with all their evil because we see in them the divine and ourselves. The hard task of making ourselves collectively better will be hard and painful to us all. It will be no easy option. The medicine will sometimes be tough but we will all share it. But the love is unconditional and it is that which kick-starts and keeps kick-starting the systems of collective security that we build up. Without that we are lost.

Notes to Chapter 7

1. F. A. Hayek: *The Constitution of Liberty* (London: Routledge and Kegan Paul, 1976), p 147.

2. Z. Bankowski and G. Mungham: *Images of Law* (London: Routledge and Kegan Paul, 1976), p 87-104.

3. H. Garfinkel: "Conditions of Successful Degradation Ceremonies", in *American Journal of Sociology*, Volume 61 (1955), pp 420-424.

4. R. M. Titmuss: *The Gift Relationship: From Human Blood to Social Policy* (London: London School of Economics, 1997).

5. Z. Bankowski, N. R. Hutton, J. J. McManus: *Lay Justice* (Edinburgh: T & T Clark, 1987).

CHAPTER 8

Double Vision

WE must now look more closely at contemporary British society in order both to see how it is and to envisage how it might be.

Having clarified our understanding of the nature of hope and of the formation of vision, having surveyed recent British history, and having examined the larger socialist and Christian traditions which have flowed from the past to the present, we now look at the present and through it to possible futures, in the light of our understanding of the structuring of generosity and the relation between love and law. Our treatment of love and law has shown that there is an inescapable dialectic. Our concept of structured generosity exhibits this dialectical mix.

A Mixed Economy

An important feature of contemporary British society is that it is in various ways a mix, that it is shot through with dialectical relations. It is not a single unified system; it is rather a field in which different and often conflicting forces are operating. In particular, it is neither a capitalist system nor a socialist system. There is at least a duality of values and structures, some of which could be described as capitalist and some as socialist. It is a 'mixed economy' and more than economy, a mixed culture and polity; however, the common use of the term 'mixed economy' is an indication that the economic manifestations of the duality are the most obvious. We now point out the ways in which our present economy is such a mix, how the 'frontier' between the two elements, capitalist and socialist, is movable in either direction, how it *has* been moved in both directions and how it *could* be moved in either.

This duality is closely connected, though not identical, with the duo, private sector and public sector. In the chapter following this one we will show that this is not the whole story, since to these two sectors must be added a third – the voluntary sector. There has recently been a rediscovery of the importance of this third sector, which belongs neither to the political/legislative/ statutory realm nor to that of markets and profits; it has been described as 'intermediate', *ie* 'below' state level and 'above' individual level. It is also associated with the term 'civil society' (*ie* not 'political society') or, in some Catholic circles, simply with the term 'society'.

But first, we look at the 'mixed economy' duality. To speak of a 'mixed' economy obviously implies that while capitalist institutions and market-profit-driven production and distribution may have a dominant role in economic life, the whole socio-economic system may be modified by and contain substantial elements of socialist values, forms of organisation, and outcomes. This might be seen as involving a series of 'frontiers of control', capable, under varying political and economic pressures, of shifting either towards more socialist systems or in the direction of what one might call unrepentant capitalism. 'Thatcherism' can be seen as an example of a substantial and many-sided shift of the 'frontier of control' within the UK's mixed economy. Changes in forms of ownership are an important dimension of such changes, but there are many other elements of socialist concern to be reviewed. Combining a number of aspects of socialist socio-economic principle and practice could be strategically important in any transition to a more socialised mixed economy.

Much of the 'ethic' involved in socialist criticism of capitalist organisation emerges from social experience of capitalist practice. Thus the persistent drive of capitalist enterprise and markets to extreme inequality in power and wealth contrasts with egalitarian and democratic citizenship concerns. The development path has involved hectic accumulation and crises, concentration of activity in particular centres and spiralling decline elsewhere (what Myrdal called 'cumulative causation'). Innovation has gone hand in hand with monopoly power, and generated the destruction and displacement of earlier products and processes. The development of workers, communities, the environment has been distorted and damaged both in development and in decline. Notably, people as workers, with their human capital of skill endowment, have been treated as 'costs', alienated through the 'wage-system' (cf the Guild Socialist criticism)[1] and subjected to a 'command' economy of coercive discipline. A persistent feature of socialist criticism has

been that the capitalist firm, its property 'rights' and its moti-
vations, neglect, disrupt and distort the social nature of the
processes involved and their wider effects. In the twentieth century
much of the so-called 'wealth creating' development has hinged
on the robber economy of extracting and not replacing the finite
resources of the globe with no regard for sustainable development.
The struggle for 'profitable' results may lead to overlapping and
waste alongside a failure to provide for all; the provision of infra-
structure services (utilities, *etc*) being an important example.
Increasingly the system has been characterised not by competition
as conventionally conceived but by the oscillations between competition, collaboration, and take-over of a limited number (hence
'oligopoly') of giant transnational firms; the issues of power and
responsibility become socially inescapable.

Socialist Criteria?

A one-dimensional socialist agenda might seek to transfer, for
example, to state ownership, the property rights that have enjoyed
such license. It is indeed important to identify where such property transfers have in the past (as in the UK) met, or may in the
future meet, specific economic and social needs. But the delin-
eation of capitalist development sketched above involved a much
wider range of issues of value and practice that have to be brought
into focus. Concentration of economic power without social
accountability raises a series of issues of social accountability
and economic regulation which connect with social democratic
political values. They also pose the question of whether power is
concentrated to be diffused later, or transformed in other ways.
The alienating and dictatorial 'wage-system' needs in response
more than an adversarial trade union system, and raises questions
of social rights and industrial democracy including gender and
other forms of discrimination. Growing inequality of wealth,
income, and access to resources forces a response which argues
from fairness and equality against exclusion.

Capitalism's failure to harness resources to meet universal social
needs and socially necessary provision for participation in the
citizenship of civil society is confronted head on with the direct
provision of massive services, and on a widening range, built round
both the needs of all and the needs of each. Damage to communities and the environment from the limited perspective of profit-

centred accounting has to be challenged and prevented in terms of enforced recognition of wider social interests. The agenda could be extended. The point is that these are not haphazard positions to adopt in face of the real nature of unrestrained capitalism; they express a coherent and cumulative sense of shared social needs and concerns. The combined force of these concerns may move towards transcending rather than modifying capitalist organisation, values and relationships. But they are clearly about changing the terms of reference within which society determines the functions of productive capital, and the responsibilities as well as the opportunities accruing to property in various forms of 'ownership'.

'According to their Needs'

Over a very large and socially critical segment of social and economic organisation in the UK the control and deployment of resources, and crucially the handling of services to users, are not subject to the values and norms of the market economy. Instead of the inequality and exclusion of 'ability to pay' these services are in substantial part (for Thatcherite market norms are being superimposed in a variety of ways, so one cannot say 'wholly') driven by the requirement for a universal and equally accessible provision related to the satisfaction of individual and social need. The range of public services provided in this way is not a static one – indeed, in all logic, it should develop and change as a dynamic economy and open debate in society produce a re-formulation of needs and how needs can best be met.

From the point of view of socialist principle and practice this range of public services is of enormous importance:

1. They exemplify and develop in practice an ethos of public service and respect for the rights and needs of all citizens. It would seem inevitable that no arbitrary limit can be placed on the sheer potential involved (eg in education to secure 'the full and free development of all'), although traditional 'professional' attitudes may seek to harness and control the values and aspirations attached to particular services.

2. They offer a process of social learning, and expectation, about equality, citizenship, and respect for a variety of needs and concerns in democratic society. They, therefore, set up, on a

large scale and in ways that impinge on all, value systems and experiences that challenge the norms of commercialism.

3. They raise inescapably the issue of the social discipline involved in accepting the transfer payments required (from taxation, much of which may fall on 'market' derived income and wealth) to enable social needs to be met more fully instead of being rationed. Finance plays a major role; the scope for redistribution away from the extreme inequalities engendered by the market is relevant here, but there are real issues of social choice to be faced through the democratic process. At least in *appearance* it may seem as if provision of such services is at the expense of individual purchasing power in the market place (in reality cutting back public services means the economy lurches towards more inequality, deprivation, and not least unemployment).

The public services and the development of future policy towards them has exceptional significance in the modern economy. The stresses and deprivation of an increasingly unequal society put additional strains on services such as health and security; more fundamental programmes for reinforcing preventive measures on illness, accidents, crime *etc*, are not as yet in place. Confusion on organisation, value systems, public accountability has to be tackled (as, too, in education). Given the information technology revolution, a greatly strengthened public system of education accessible through life, linked with a coherent communication system using advanced technology has become a central requirement for future social and economic development. The choice between a democratised, social needs based, approach to those questions and the piecemeal, exploitative, approach of capitalist enterprise is of massive importance.

In the case of such public services as school education, health services, and security services, the provision for individual and social needs is largely financed from general taxation. In large part too the organisational control and ownership rests with public authorities (though Thatcherism has developed more autonomous forms of 'trust' organisation in health). In further and higher education the bulk of the financing comes from state funds, fed through public agencies on criteria that seek to establish priorities and norms of provision while also attempting to encourage efficiency and quality; but the providing agencies are based on trusts or forms of charter that reach back to pre-capitalist collegiate forms. In other words, there are choices that may be made in the means of pursuing 'needs' based provision, and the extent of the state finance.

Other important public services may be able to meet social needs while raising a significant proportion of the revenue required to maintain and develop the service. Important examples would be 'social' housing provision and contributions from rent revenue (though this in turn may be only partly paid by the occupier and partly financed by public funds related to the 'means' of the occupier'); 'public' transport, with significant subsidies both from central and from local authorities (making it the more unfortunate that a spurious and dis-integrated 'private' enterprise should have been interpolated in rail operation to extract a profit slice). An excellent example of publicly accountable 'needs'-based provision being compatible with 'affordable' charges for the service is our oldest national utility, the post office. This may yet come under threat from European pressures to challenge the monopoly that simplifies and reduces its operating costs.

There are, or course, a range of public utility industries and services, from electricity to telecommunication, which operate now as private sector companies but come under very extensive regulation and strict licence requirements. This previously nationalised sector still carries an important range of social responsibilities relating to social and individual needs. These include 'universal service' obligations, at least on the dominant firms, to meet all reasonable demands for the service, to provide domestic users with uniform averaged tariffs without discrimination, to maintain adequate investment to meet changing levels of demand, and so on. This is an area of some social tension and challenge (thus increased disconnections following privatisation have been vigorously challenged, and the utilities have been made to retreat from such anti-social pressures). Price controls have in many cases left utility companies with excessive profits, and the main benefits of price control have been secured by business users rather than small consumers. The point, however, is that significant issues of social – and in essence, socialist – policy are contested across vast 'infra-structure' industries, with fair and 'affordable' access for all as a key objective of social responsibility and the regulatory process. In the European Union the notion of 'social' policy has been extended from a wide range of industrial relations and employment practices to include such issues of 'universal service' commitments. The matters at stake are not only material ones, but concern not only publicly accountable regulation, but principles of much wider consultation in society, of searching investigation and provision of key information, of representation of consumer and employee interests, and of special provision and concern for the disadvantaged.

The role of publicly organised enterprises and services, at local community/governmental level and regionally (through consortia of local authorities), is also of considerable – and almost certainly increasing – importance. Shared community resources, and improved environmental access, for creativity and participation as well as for recreation, are determinants of the social quality of life. For this and other reasons, public transport services need to be extended and made affordable, to reflect principles of provision according to social needs and wider access (and away from the distortions and ever higher social costs of unregulated private transport). Of course, such socialised provision does involve reconciling a diverse range of social needs and concerns: thus, Manchester airport (a consortium of ten local authorities) with planned expansion and development, which (*inter alia*) may generate many thousand additional jobs, has to seek to satisfy environmental responsibilities and concerns.

The process of developing more socialised organisations and objectives is not only a matter of direct public, or manifestly social, provision, but of operating within an extending range of accepted – and where necessary enforced – social responsibilities, identified through democratic processes and legal responsibility. This wider process calls for more systematic analysis.

About Social Responsibility

It is crucial for the well-being of society that there should be a developing framework of economic and social responsibilities that have to be accepted and operated by economic enterprises. The responsibilities are likely to be more far-reaching so far as large enterprises are concerned since questions of monopoly power, standard setting, and influence on innovation are more directly involved.

This assertion of social responsibility should not be seen as 'interference' with rational economic allocation and efficiency but rather the necessary condition for fully rational choice. The wider social costs and benefits involved in enterprise production and distribution need to be brought within the enterprise's accounts and development decisions (the partial accountability that only looks at costs directly encountered within the firm and only at its revenues will otherwise send the wrong signals). In so far as such social costs/benefits are quantified and brought into business accounts and reports (*eg* through taxes or levies, through subsidies or rebates), then we can think of the accountancy or audit involved as more fully socialised. Wider access to and debate about such social auditing is an important contribution to social learning. The factors involved in such social costs/benefits include such matters as environmental concerns and the development of the human resources involved.

But there will be issues of social values and needs that are not readily quantifiable, or which are so clearly undesirable (as with aspects of pollution, or neglect of safety) as to be prohibited or subject to other forms of direct 'control', such as regulatory agencies. Examples would be misuse of market power (control of monopoly power and behaviour; consumer protection; discriminatory practices). Positive expression of social values may take the form of legislative/regulatory requirements to recognise employee or consumer rights, individual and collective, or provision for employee benefits and their responsible management (occupational pensions as an example).

Development of such frameworks of social responsibility could in their turn be socially divisive if they operated through inadequately accountable state agencies or through elaborate (and slow and expensive) legal processes. This suggests that socialist criteria would emphasise participatory democracy and openness in developing, operating, and monitoring what is done in the name of the social responsibilities of business. Accountability is a key concept, within the economic organisation to shareholders and employees, externally to the relevant communities and consumers.

It is worth emphasising that such regulatory agendas are far from being the exclusive concern of 'sovereign' states. Since the power centres of capitalist business are transnational, the effective recognition and implementation of social responsibilities call for regulatory principles, agencies, and legislative practice which involve the extensive sharing of state sovereignty. An example of this is the European Union with the slow development of regulations governing business behaviour in the 'single market', as well as underpinning the individual and collective rights of workers.

Within the 'sovereign' state, local, regional, and distinctive national democratic processes and government can connect the communities that people identify with to the development and implementation of social responsibilities. This is not only a process involving regulatory protection but one that can involve sharing in the opportunities and responsibilities of future economic and social development and change.

Forms of Common Ownership in the Mixed Economy

More analysis and discussion is needed as to the evaluation of past and present experience of common ownership in mixed economies such as the UK. Such analysis may influence future choices as to the organisational forms and objectives of common and public ownership in the future. Certainly, experiment and monitoring should be seen as a natural part of the evolution of common ownership. Here, all that is attempted is a somewhat schematic listing of a variety of forms, and some brief comments on aspects of UK experience.

Some reference has been made earlier to the particular role played by 'nationalised industries' in post-war UK experience of public ownership. Indeed, these for many years appeared as the dominant form, and recognition of the importance of other forms of common ownership and their potential (such as mutual and co-operative organisation) was all too muted. But some account of the experience of nationalisation may not be out of place.

The 'nationalised industry' was particularly influenced by business concern with efficient operation of utility services. Given the potential gains of a single integrated system to provide fully extensive utility services, a number of studies had built up the case for taking over both public (local government) and private operators and giving a public corporation the task of complete re-organisation. This applied to electricity and to gas and rail. It produced an emphasis on strong centralisation. In water it meant pursuing regional organisation. Probably the reason this was not envisaged as a function for a government department was the massive investment involved. This, in turn, meant that the public industries were not only characterised by co-ordinated centralised administration but also by a shift to capital intensity and a large scale displacement of manual labour.

Linked with this forceful re-organisation was at least a partial recognition of the need to extend provision to serve more people and communities (*eg* rural electrification), and to strengthen productive capacity and so avoid a constraint on national economic growth. This latter concern was relevant to the belated nationalisation of steel. It also stimulated the removal of telecommunications and posts from direct departmental control to a public corporation form, and then the separation off of telecommunications.

This was hardly a pattern of development that could be continued unchanged for a long period without tension, and not one that could be more widely adopted. The legislative structures rested too heavily on monopoly rather than enterprise and dynamic change. The centralisation could well have been relaxed and reconsidered. Formal structures of accountability contrasted with the reality of blurred relationships, and concealed intervention, between government departments and the public corporations. In particular the Treasury emerged as a major, and arbitrary and 'short-termist', controller of investment, pricing, and financial balances. The notion of long term planned development was distorted and undermined. Such a pattern limited the scope for positive industrial democracy, or for open consultation on ordinary consumers' needs and choices.

All of this makes clear that there is substantially more to objectives of socialising aspects of production and services than the formal process of transfer of ownership. The relationship between functional priorities and forms of organisation have to be reviewed and re-thought in dynamic conditions. Scope for participation in management and control by political communities, workers, and consumers has to be explored and tested. The social objectives (especially those concerned with wider and affordable access) have to be more explicitly addressed in doing so. This implies a variety of forms and scale of collective ownership, and of legislative support and influence, as well as variety in the forms of accountability, stakeholder participation and trusteeship.

The forms that common ownership may take are many. We draw attention to the following six.

Direct Governmental Administration

This may mean local government, regional government (when it exists), and national government. In particular, there may be a need for 'hybrids' (eg consortia of local authorities), though here some form of subsidiary organisation may operate. This has been important in education and housing at local government level. Handling of police services has involved an element of shared control. At national government level, the health service has operated through directly appointed boards, but without the degree of separation of public corporations. Not surprisingly, defence has also operated as a central government function. The Post Office operated as a central government department for most of its existence and was only given the public corporation form in the UK in the late 1960s.

Public Corporations

These are still a significant type. They may be particularly useful in managing integrated basic economic activities of an infra-structure kind (such as rail, postal, utility grids). In the UK there is a Housing Corporation with a range of social housing functions; this may represent a device of the government to distance local authorities from such active development of the housing stock; a consortium of local authorities on a regional or sub-regional basis might be more directly democratic in accountability and more connected with the specifics of local community needs. In the utility field, co-ordination of regional energy plcs – instead of separation into gas/electricity/etc – might be more useful than the previous corporation structure, or than the present regulatory regime in Britain.

'Social Ownership'

Such as Trusts (eg National Trust); this is a form that could be encouraged and widely developed. The flexible development of 'social' housing might use such a form. Where there are a variety of social views and opinions, 'Trusts' that are not profit-orien-tated may be socially preferable to the kind of commercial con-centrations of power that have emerged in the media.

Co-operatives and Mutual Societies

Co-operatives may have been in retreat in the retail trade sector, in face of the vast economies of scale of the multiples, but they constitute a varied and experienced range of activities, eg in agricultural supply and purchasing. A fresh look at the potential for employment creation and viable development through the co-operative form is called for. Mutual societies, such as building societies and credit unions, have great potential in handling a variety of finance and credit needs of ordinary households and groups of employees or people in localities or other forms of association with a common bond of interests. Here too there should be thought as to how to stimulate their internal democracy, improve their communication, provide them with more support services, and identify new patterns of shared objective that can make effective use of their form of shared ownership and control.

Debate around revised and more sympathetic legislation to encourage the retention and extension of 'mutual' organisation could be important. Recent moves by commercial banks and by the management of building societies to persuade members in mutual societies to sell-out their mutual rights (and change into conventional profit-centred joint-stock companies) should be resisted. The existing mutuals (such as Nationwide) can fight back by offering better terms to borrowers and higher rates to lenders than their joint-stock rivals, who have interposed the acquisitive interests of profit-taking between the two.

Workers' Capital Funds (especially Pension Funds)

The particular significance of the pension funds is that they manage, as trustees, members' funds that are *deferred pay transformed into capital*. In the UK their scale and the deployment of their assets is of enormous significance – but their potential role is far greater. In recent years their total assets have reached a market value of around £500 billion (that is, £500,000 million); most significantly, over half of these take the form of equity share holdings in UK companies. It has been estimated that this combined share ownership of the UK pension funds represents around one-third of all UK company equity capital. Other 'institutional' shareowners, notably insurance companies, between them account for another third of the total. Since the mid 1970s alone the share of total UK equity capital held by the pension funds has doubled, while that held by 'persons' has halved.

The pension funds have in the UK around eleven million worker contributors and millions of retired-worker recipients. Collectively these workers 'by hand and brain' are the most massive and rapidly growing force in 'ownership' in UK industry, commerce and finance. The social potential of that ownership has not yet been realised. Even democratic control and membership accountability within the funds is inadequate. Within the right legislative framework these funds could operate with democratic and socially responsible guidelines, and with the full participation of the workers collectively involved. The 'trustee' role, and the accountability that needs to go with that, is highly important. These organisations break down through shared ownership of capital the great divide between labour and capital in industrial society. The *active* use by such funds of their massive combined stakes in equity holdings could change the social role of shareholders and shareholding (for instance in forcing the pace of better 'governance' of joint-stock companies).

The historic irony is that these funds grew out of self-interest of the senior administrative and managerial – including directorial – personnel of big companies; they did not want the worst features of the wage system to apply to themselves, so asset-backed 'funded' pension schemes developed for them, helped by a priv-ileged tax position for such funds. The base of participation widened over time, with growing trade union understanding of what was at stake. It may seem an unusual starting point for a break-through from the old exploitative wage system towards a more socialised recognition of employees' rights and needs, and away from previously polarised property relationships. But the pension fund system still bears the marks of its inegalitarian origins (earlier discrimination between 'staff' and manual workers; unfair treatment of those who left – or were dismissed – long before retirement age). For many part-time women workers discrimi-nation still left them outside this particular transcendence of the old wage-system – or did until the social responsibilities and employee rights enforced through new European institutions came to assist in their rescue.

Joint-Stock Companies

Public ownership has on many occasions used the joint-stock plc form, sometimes operating under a state holding company or agency. This was important in the 1960s/1970s when a number of significant UK firms were faced with bankruptcy and extinction, which would have involved major damage to the economy through loss of exports, collapse of major employment bases, *etc.* The 'rescue' of Rolls Royce, Leyland *etc*, created an opportunity for re-organisation under state ownership and on a more advanced and efficient basis. The re-structuring was the historic function that such state ownership performed. State ownership in these conditions could be seen as continuing on a long term basis, or involving subsequent re-flotation as a commercial company. The latter approach involves a changing portfolio of publicly owned companies going through a rehabilitation process.

More widely, the joint-stock form does represent to a limited extent a recognition of the social – as against purely private – organisation and function of capital. Developments in company legislation, social regulation, and new patterns of shareholding activity, could move this form of property organisation towards a more socially involved and participatory use and control of capital, bringing employees, shareholders, and local communities into more active representation and constructive roles in the productive use of capital.

It is already possible to see a growing sense of the importance of an active use of 'institutional' (especially pension fund) shareholder influence on company policy and 'governance'. Certainly the old passivity of these large scale 'institutional' equity holdings was socially indefensible and left so-called 'private ownership' as an empty box category in an economic system steered by largely non-accountable top executives of giant firms. So we should greet the British TUCs recent issue of 'Guidelines' on shareholder voting for the member trustees on the boards of pension funds as a welcome straw in the wind. Consciously designed to strengthen the current emphasis on active fund intervention through combined shareholding pressure, the guidelines were drafted for the TUC by Pensions Investment Research Consultants, an organisation which has for some time been working with 'like-minded' pension funds of progressive local authorities to develop a new force for socially responsible ownership.

But if the participatory rights and powers of shareholders as 'stakeholders' in the joint-stock company are to be emphasised and made effective, thus giving, in the case of pension funds, real social function to their social ownership, so too should there be emphasis on the rights and responsibilities of other stakeholders notably the employees who have a very direct concern in company development. Pension fund trustees exercising shareholding rights on behalf of their (worker) members should be complemented by representatives of the company's employees in an evolving process of shared participation, co-determination, within the form of the joint-stock company. Reform of company law for such purposes should be seen as part of a socialist agenda to strengthen the rights, and to develop the representativeness, of social ownership.

Note to Chapter 8

1. See G. D. H. Cole: *Self Government in Industry*, p 154-155 – 'wages paid only when it is profitable to the capitalist to employ labour' ... 'the wage-worker surrenders all control over the organisation of production' and 'all claim upon the product of labour'.

CHAPTER 9

Treble Vision

The Third Force

Much of traditional socialist rhetoric has focussed on conflicts between public and private sectors. The major objective was to bring the 'commanding heights' of the economy from private hands into public control, ensuring democratic accountability and responsiveness to need rather than the profit motive. Much of the rethinking on the left (as already indicated) has been in light of the realisation that the practice of nationalisation has not only involved other problems but also substantially failed to deliver on the stated objectives. While socialist thought may now have gone beyond the simplistic 'public good/private bad' slogans of the past (in order, as seen above, to hold on to the underlying values and vision), there is still a major focus of concern on the way the public sector works and on the role of the state. Yet there is an emerging concern that this, in itself, is not enough.

Churches too, while apparently belonging more naturally on the 'private' side of the great divide, have historically sought, from the time of Constantine, an alliance with the state in some form, usually as a lever of power. The various 'national', 'established' or 'state' churches, which remain part of the constitutional structure of several Western European countries, represent not quite an incorporation into the public sector but at least a tradition of commitment and concern for what goes on there. Here, too, there is unease within as well as outwith the churches about this aspect of the tradition.

Both Christian and socialist traditions, therefore, might be seen as ready to embrace the voluntary sector as an attractive option. Although it is one which may at times have disappeared between the two stools of public and private, it is an area to which both traditions have made important contributions from the co-operative movements and Victorian charitable societies to the pressure groups and community projects of today (as evidenced by the

Kirk's Priority Areas Fund). It may also be seen as an option which avoids some of the difficulties encountered by both with the public sector but if we are to see the activities of the voluntary sector as vital ingredients of our vision, it cannot be as a means of dodging the crucial issues of the public/private debate. That way lies a vision that has lost touch with reality.

However, it is in their engagement with reality at its most immediate and painful that the varied activities of this third force offer some seeds of hope. Civil society, we are slowly learning, is much wider than the political structures upon which we have concentrated. Hope that is to avoid being utopian demands not spectators who wait and quinquennially vote but participants who start to engage with the injustices they encounter and build alternatives together (as citizens in a community rather than subjects of a system). Such a participative citizenship represents a radical alternative to both the brave new entrepreneurial individuals of the right and the pew or production-line fodder of more monolithic constructs; it is in the voluntary sector that such things can be glimpsed already happening.

To recognise that there are wider issues of power and justice setting the context for what goes on is not, therefore, to deny that the voluntary sector has a major role in any construct of social justice, social renewal and therefore social vision. We encountered this, in conversations with community activists in Easterhouse, as a very positive and encouraging sense of a community bustling with a range of action groups, support groups *etc*, which are lively enough to have a culture of their own. Through the experience of listening to the excitement, sense of achievement and commitment of an overlapping network of people, both volunteers and employees of funded projects, there was a definite sense of a community trying to reshape itself.

The role of the voluntary sector has expanded substantially in recent years and is likely to continue to do so. The reason for that expansion has, in some respects, come from two kinds of failure. On the right, market forces have failed to protect the weak and the non-commercial; on the left, centralised state socialism has often proved unresponsive to the great variety and complexity of human needs. One more specifically avowed justification for voluntary sector growth has been the Conservatives' strategy of cutting back the public sector; shifting service delivery from public to private sector may have been the ideologically preferred option, but this has not always been viable and such voluntary sector agencies as housing associations have offered an inter-mediate solution. The growing inadequacy of public services (whether perceived as inevitably characteristic of state provision or as the result of ideologically motivated cut-backs) may also spur the development of voluntary services to fill the gap.

One characteristic we found in Easterhouse was a sense that long-term avowedly socialist local government, which has not delivered, which remains remote and which leaves folk feeling powerless rather than empowered, has undermined faith both in the socialist vision and in the ability to achieve meaningful change by means of conventional party politics. People who have learned a distrust of grand political schemes and of national and local government as vehicles of positive change are joining single-issue campaigns and pressure groups where they feel injustice (although the learning experience of such involvement, and the networking among such groups may lead to a broadening of their involvement).

Another factor in voluntary sector growth has been the expan-sion of the 'social space' in which such groups operate. We cannot expect that the social space opened up by the retreat of the old dominance of full-time work in adult life can be substantially filled either by state-provided, professionally delivered services or by private, profit-pursuing enterprise. Into the space left by the decline in full-time work (particularly in areas of deprivation) and the absence of alternatives, the voluntary sector has grown.

Defining and Describing the Voluntary Sector

The pace and diversity of this expansion leaves serious problems of definition. We can start with voluntary action, *ie* action in pursuit of some social or public good, freely undertaken or led by people without material reward. When voluntary action becomes formally organised, it generally results in the paid employment of people to maintain and promote its services, but the voluntary organisation remains distinct from the private sector because it is a non-profit organisation, with volunteer workers as well as paid, direction by an unpaid management board, and objectives in terms of a social 'good'. Yet some groups (*eg* self-help groups and recreational or sports clubs) don't seem to fit such a definition naturally. And the concept of a (registered) charity is also problematic in terms of catering for the highly privileged (as in 'public' schools) or the restrictions placed by government regulators on 'political' campaigning. The Scottish Council for Voluntary Organisations has argued for a definition in terms of 'Public Benefit Organisation', but, while this may be helpful in terms of equity in tax advantages, the sector's strengths of flexibility and diversity may push it beyond comprehensive definition.

It is important to note that there may well be important elements of state funding (urban programme, lottery finance, *etc*) involved without changing the locus of groups within the voluntary sector; neither are elements of entrepreneurial initiative or some revenue generation to be seen as moving such groups into the private sector. There are, however, considerable problems arising as the application for funds requires certain management styles, business plans *etc*, and the increasingly contractual nature of relationships with national and local government may also threaten the essential freedom and diversity of voluntary groups.

In clarifying the voluntary sector role, we need to look at the strengths and weaknesses of the three sectors. The public sector can offer the classic advantages of legally-guaranteed equality of treatment, consistent standards, secure and predictable resources and electoral democratic accountability. It also has the related weaknesses of rigidity, slowness of response and electoral accountability (the last being both advantage and disadvantage, helping to force a response in relation to legitimate problems or inhibiting a response to the needs of vulnerable minorities). The public sector is the appropriate vehicle for the delivery of basic services and benefits, and as such has a cherished position for socialists for whom its advantages are crucial dimensions of service provision.

The private sector can be innovative, enterprising and efficient; it is effective in providing for many consumer needs when these are equipped with purchasing power. But the market reflects, and tends to exploit and widen, the great inequalities in society; it is often short-sighted and unintelligent. For the right, its (claimed) values of efficiency outweigh the disadvantages as a deliverer of services.

Strengths and Weaknesses

What, then, are the strengths of the voluntary sector? It can represent the interests of many groups who are themselves neither 'important' (or popular) in the political system nor endowed with the purchasing power to be influential in the market. It is free to be innovative, to pioneer new developments without all the con-

straints of profitability or public bureaucracy. It provides a channel
for the concerns, the energy and talents of a large section of the
public to contribute to the common good; that is, it is an area
where people not only feel that their involvement can make a
difference but also that they can begin to take control over areas
of their own lives and that of their communities. Their diversity is
of the utmost importance in an increasingly plural culture, where
solutions to problems are more likely to be found by harnessing
the perspectives, urgencies and skills of those who come at the
problems from different directions.

This is particularly so where the concern is likely to be a
minority one which parties are unlikely to see electoral gain in
pursuing; who will be the party for the Down's Syndrome child,
the refugee, the ex-prisoner? There is a real possibility for a genuine
Rainbow Coalition to emerge, complementing the conventional
part-led political democracy, helping to restore faith in the wider
political processes and both conscientising and supporting those
who become involved. As already noted, this freedom and flexibility is under threat. If the voluntary sector takes on too much
routine responsibility for the provision of services, it risks becoming
a partial replacement for the public sector without the same security of resources and with the danger of having its independence
undermined. These dangers, and the vulnerability of a voluntary
sector to restraints on local government finance (as monitored by
SCVO in terms of the impact of constraints on the new councils)
and to such changes in policy as the national lottery (whose effect
has been to substitute quango direction of funds for more traditional fund-raising by charities *etc*), may well fuel some suspicion
of the voluntary sector.

Views from the Traditions

Certainly, there has been some ambivalence in the socialist tradition towards such (especially charitable) groups. On the one hand,
mutual associations, friendly societies, co-operatives, trade unions
and campaigning groups have had a key role in the socialist
movement (before political parties came to predominate); on the
other, the great thrust of twentieth century social democracy has
been away from the vicissitudes and arbitrariness of charity
towards entitlement and equality of treatment.

While many social concerns have found, historically, a voice and the mobilisation of support and care through voluntary groups, the successful transition to state provision of that care has been a hard-fought battle. Suspicion of a move back toward the private sector may be inflamed by the Right's agenda of desire to deconstruct the public sector and apparent lack of commitment to those most in need of its services and least able to buy them from the private sector. But the charities do not want charity to substitute for entitlement; they want charity to strengthen entitlement and supplement it. The voluntary sector may, then, bite the right hand which offers them patronage, but the left cannot be complacent. They have to come to a positive accommodation with the sector with which they have often been ill at ease. That sector exists, has expanded, and enjoys public support; there is a growing number of people with a professional vested interest in it, and many others who have learned to trust it more than either of the other sectors. The 'mixed economy of care' may be an attempt by a Conservative government to get services on the cheap and undermine the public sector, but, promoted constructively, it has some real advantage in offering variety and innovation (so long as these are not stifled by the contract culture). The sector is more in tune with centre/left values than with those of the right, but much more has to be done to fit it into a framework of public service provision of which the left can be genuinely supportive. 'Partnership' emerges painfully out of social need, constrained resources and inadequate provision, but it can none the less be part of a socialist vision for the future, not least because it is one which is attractive to many who in a previous generation might have been expected to rally to the socialist cause.

Perhaps a national church may have historically seen itself as part as the public sector, and there may be a hangover of sympathy for that sector in the Kirk today. But in late twentieth century Scotland, the churches themselves may be seen as belonging to the voluntary sector, albeit with an older self-understanding dominant in their thinking over the bustling networks of other participants in local voluntary sector forums. Such initiatives as the Kirk's recent Priority Areas Fund, seeking partnerships with other voluntary groups in responding to community needs (as well as in seeking mixed funding for such ventures) suggest that things may be changing. Congregations in these areas, often feeling a sense of being embattled and struggling (in contrast with 'successful' suburban churches with their own nostalgia-enhanced past) may have a great deal to gain from such engagement (in terms of mutual support, encouragement and credibility) as well as resources and insights to offer from the tradition. Though small in relative numbers, they can still mobilise significant voluntary people-power to causes to which they are committed (as some have shown, for example, in leading the way in the formation of Credit Unions).

The element of Christian tradition which seems most relevant here is the currently fashionable one of subsidiarity, rooted in Catholic social teaching but finding new life in the European debate. What the voluntary sector seems to achieve more effectively than national or local government is a sense of empowerment and appropriate control by members of a local community over the life of that community. Sometimes against the bureaucratic opposition of 'real' municipal socialism, community groups are harnessing energy and vision as well as giving a sense of participation lacking in mainstream party politics.

Uncomfortable Presence or Source of Hope?

Recognition of the value and the increased role of this sector can be an important ingredient of social vision. Voluntary organisations – across their variety – have an almost infinite capacity to express particular interests and aspirations, and to reflect a range of cultures (both in value systems and organisational modes), which are beyond the possibilities of the public sector. Voluntary organisation also has an astonishing capacity for building connections, all the way from the local to the international. It can, and does, follow through its concerns (if it believes in one world it can advance to one world). It can do so not through hierarchy that dis-esteems the local, but through an immense variety of governmental and connective processes (charged with the new energy of an attractive new information technology). In contrast, the state's processes of operation are substantially confined to national and local government, with an awkwardness even there about the sharing of resources and responsibilities. We should not underrate the voluntary sector's ability to transcend.

As noted above, this has a community-building function in several dimensions; not least of these is the educational dimension of participation (with new and varied groups taking on that function previously most prominently carried out within the trade unions) and of the research spawned and carried out by such groups. For an older (male?) model, serving on the playgroup committee may not seem a key role in the revolution, but in terms of growth in awareness and skills of advocacy and negotiation it should not be sneered at.

This dimension may be seen as threatened by the growing 'professionalism' within the voluntary sector. While voluntary work (*ie* unpaid effort) is often seen as the essence of this sector, organising the consistent delivery of a service, raising regular income, providing specialist advice and comment cannot be done without paid, full-time staffing. The more the sector is drawn into contracting for services, the more they must have reliable, predictable, skilled staff. Indeed, a growing professionalism is central to the growth of unpaid volunteering (something the churches should readily recognise), and as more people build up experience and skills within different parts of the sector a network is already developing, with the advantages of a growing skills base and the disadvantages of a degree of conservatism and possible exclusivism. While the 'professional' in a voluntary organisation may be deploying his or her skills in the service of the organisations goals, that may shade into a dominating hierarchy of esteem. Further, 'professional' delivery of services may start to displace the community self-help which is one of the characteristic strengths of the voluntary sector.

What is clear is that the cherished polarities of public and private sectors are no longer viable as the exclusive dimensions of a social vision, particularly one which seeks to build communities and nourish hope. Among the diversities of the voluntary sector, this is already happening, and it would be tragic if the consequences of the contract culture or of the attractions of a soft target for local authorities strapped for cash were to undermine its significance and effectiveness. We are, therefore, glad to find glimpses of our vision taking shape in the voluntary sector (see below), not as a second-best to the macro-scale changes that are also needed, but as important contributions to the lives of communities and real signs of hope; these, we believe, are some of the places where it is happening.

CHAPTER 10

Vision Formation

IN conclusion, we do not present a portrait of the 'good society' but offer only materials and methods for good social sketching; for it is implicit, both in our concept of hope not as a final destination but as a journey which never ends and in our concept of justice not as a stable state but as a corrective act which requires constant repetition, that vision formation is re-formation — *ie* a constantly repeated and renewed process. So we offer some hints, some theses and some glimpses, to assist such vision formation.

Some Hints

Vision formation is irreducibly plural, in two ways. It is so, first, in that its horizon is ever-expanding. When any horizon is reached, it becomes the vantage point for viewing a further horizon, and so the process of vision formation goes on. Vision formation is plural, secondly, in that it is related to the irreducible plurality of people, with their many different definitions of their needs and priorities, in Gramsci's terms, the 'spontaneous philosophies of everyday life'.

This emphasis on process rather than state, and on plurality rather than singularity, puts us at a distance from utopian thinking, both of the kind which Marx criticised, namely as detached from the specific dynamics of historical process, and of the kind in which many, including many Marxists, have believed, namely as the single, ultimate, absolute, good society.

Vision formation also avoids several common antitheses. For example, it does not set individual and social fulfilment over against each other, for, as we have sought to show, individual autonomy and social mutuality are interdependent, there being no autonomy without mutuality and no mutuality without autonomy. As we have also sought to show, personal act and social structure, though their relation is complex, do form a single story, making the innermost personal biography and the outermost social historiography inseparable.

No more does vision formation set moral fulfilment and material fulfilment over against one another, both morality and materiality being pervasive features of the very structure of human existence. This rules out therefore the not uncommon antithesis between moral issues and economic ones. Moreover, within the economic field, vision formation does not set production and distribution over against one another, or fall into the error of suggesting that wealth production is a capitalist preserve and wealth distribution a socialist preserve. Similarly, it does not set production and consumption over against one another or focus too exclusively, as socialist tradition has tended to do, on the human being as producer to the neglect of the human being as consumer.

The focus of vision formation is global, in several senses:

It is global, first, in that it includes all human beings and is not to be confined to any one group of them such as a nation; in other words, it is 'ecumenical', *ie* for all inhabitants. It is global second, in that it includes the non-human with the human elements of the planet; in other words, it is 'ecological', *ie* for the whole habitat. It is global, third, in the sense that it involves styles of living and acting which are universalisable, *ie* avoiding practices in which some can achieve the ends only by preventing others from doing so. Thus it is not competitive in the exploitative sense; it does not involve a zero-sum game, as the Thatcherite formula does.

However, it is not universal in the sense in which the universal abstracts from the particular. Our whole treatment of law and love has stressed the centrality of the particular and indeed the dialectic between the particularity and uniqueness of the spontaneous action of love and generosity and the universality and rationality of law and justice. Nor is it global in the sense of giving primacy to what happens at global level, thus rendering what happens at more local levels subordinate to or derivative from the global level. For it is non-hierarchical, having neither the singularity nor the mechanistic connectedness of 'hierarchy' (in its generalised and secularised sense). For it enshrines 'subsidiarity', with both the multiplicity of forms and levels of social unit which that term implies and their independence of one another. This means that it is not 'top-down', but also that it is not 'bottom up', for it gives primacy neither to the global nor to the local and therefore not to either direction of devolution, 'downwards', or 'upwards'. Plurality in independence precludes both. For similar reasons, it does not give primacy to either the public or the private or the voluntary sector; it is not either 'statist' or 'marketist' or 'voluntarist'.

Rejecting these 'either/ors' in favour of the corresponding 'both/ands', vision formation is confronted with a number of dialectics leading to dilemmas and conflicts. It is not possible in advance to say how these dilemmas and conflicts could and should be resolved, eg between what emanates from the different levels of social unit, global, national, regional and local; or between what emanates from the different sectors, public, private and voluntary; or between what emanates from the multiplicity within each. Negotiation between such conflicting beliefs, aspirations and interests is presumably the art of politics.

Above all, vision formation should be guided by the principal propositions of this book, which we now summarise in the following ten theses.

Some Theses

We suggest the following:

1. *That the hope that we need to act must be transformative and bring the possibility of a different future into the present.*
   We need hope to act but that hope must be able to be distinguished from false hopes. The way we argue for this is to see true hope as something that is transformative and which opens up the possibilities for the future and does not just re create the world as it is now and defend it. The vision that gives us hope is not to be seen as a destination, rather as a way of transforming our present day activities – our actions led by vision bring the future into the present. Thus we act our hope.

2. *That vision does not free us from the possibility of error – to have a transformative vision does not make for safety or security.*
   Vision is not a blueprint from which we can accurately read off what to do. Policy and decision making will never be easy. But the way we will truly fail is if we do not have the courage to risk but merely try to ensure that our policies are not out of line with what people want. At the same time genuine transformation must be realistic and start from where we are. Radical realism is not easy.

3. *That the individual and the collective are linked in the sense that the individual act is a collective act and a collective act is an individual one.*
    This is not a claim that what you do in your individual life is a reflection also of your general politics. It is about how you encounter the general; how what you do in those situations is your general politics. The conditions of collective rationality are that we individually act and risk ourselves for the collective outcome. It is the individual act of love and risk that sparks off collective welfare.

4. *That a society characterised by structured generosity depends on structures being renewed by the experience of individual acts of love.*
    The rationality of welfare provision emerges out of, and must constantly be renewed by, other-than-rational acts of individual love which demonstrate simultaneously the rationality and the irrationality of the system. In such other-than-rational acts of love the giver is shown to be vulnerable like the receiver, and both are changed. Risk and vulnerability counter the culture of contentment, challenge the claims of existing structures and demand their renewal.

5. *That a society characterised by structured generosity does not choose between welfare and market principles but holds them in a creative tension.*
    We hold that the current debate about these principles is based on the false dichotomy which holds that 'more' of one means 'less' of the other. More fruitful grounds for debate lie in questions of when which principle should apply, how the two principles may combine in different circumstances and how each principle may refine the other. A society characterised by structured generosity both challenges the consonance of welfare provision with the demonstration of individual choices expressed in the market, and challenges the morality of the market with the demonstration of needs inexpressible in the market.

6. *That a society characterised by structured generosity has both a high view of human possibility and a sense of the fragility and conditionality of human goodness.*
    Hope, an imagining that the individual and collective future could be morally better, is an essential component of fully human life. Some of humanity's worst inhumanities have

been committed in the name of hope. A society characterised by structured generosity fosters hopes, engages in critical dialogues between competing hopes, develops through hopes but is not in thrall to a hope which becomes self defeating through universalising itself.

7. *That the assumption that all human relationships can be defined in terms of contracts is reductionist and destructive; 'covenant' not only describes a richer relationship but also reflects the dimension of trust without which eventually even contractual relationships become impossible.* Relationships defined solely in terms of contracts lack a commitment to the relationship, beyond the particular contractual purpose. They cannot therefore deal adequately with the mixture of power and responsibility which is crucial to the formation of communities. The justified reaction against social forms of control without responsibility is inadequate if it merely substitutes the constraints of the market. In the real world, neither power nor responsibility can exist in a vacuum, nor in the artificial environment of a contracted relationship; they demand the mutual commitment of covenanted relationships which the market can (and inevitably does) reflect but cannot ultimately define.

8. *That the even-handed, blind, contractual justice of weighing scales is inadequate; justice is about righting wrongs that are destructive of community — it is therefore relational, creative, participative and restorative.* The Biblical insight, that 'an eye for an eye' is not sufficient to build justice, leads towards an understanding of forgiveness as part of the dynamic of justice. The Jubilee paradigm of justice through forgiveness of debts points to a vision of justice not as a static, ideal state, but as interventions continually required to stop injustice building on injustice. It is therefore not about final solutions (real or imagined), but about an ongoing process which deals with the realities of relationships; not, therefore, about an engineered perfection but about participation in change that knows both the urgency of what must be done and the limits of what can be done.

9. *That justice must retain dimensions both of solidarity and of free creativity.* While equality is a key ingredient in any attempt to seek justice, equality and solidarity defeat their own purposes if

they are not oriented toward the free expression of human creativity which is a key value in both Christian and socialist tradition. Inevitable tensions between these dimensions should not be allowed to skew thinking towards the lack of realism that seeks one through extinguishing the other. Equality and uniformity are not identical, though it has regularly suited those who have an interest in resisting the former to confuse it with the latter.

10. *That vision formation is the formation of many visions, not of a single vision.*

This is not only because of the transcendent and transformative nature of hope which eludes prediction, exceeds imagination and so requires cumulative evocative stories rather than a single definitive blueprint, but also because of the irreducible and enriching plurality and diversity of human beings and their creativity. It is not just that there are many times and places and each of us lives in a particular time and place (or at most a few places) and therefore that different geographical, historical and social perspectives need to be put together to overcome the limitations of any one person's or group's perspective. It is more positive than that. It is that each person is highly creative (though that creativity may be largely suppressed by social forces), that their creativity is an expression of the uniqueness both of their individual identity and of their many communal identities, and that the combined wealth of all such creativities is required for vision formation.

Unity in Diversity

This prospect of many visions from many visionaries – our last thesis – is an untidy one. It does not mean fragmentation or relativisation. It does mean however that a new political art requires to be developed, namely the ability to discern unity within the diversity – not the scissors-and-paste unity of putting pieces together as in the political conference practice of 'compositing', nor yet the reductive unity of eliciting common abstract principles, but rather the finding of resonances between the many visions through the maintenance of a continuing dialogue.

In view of this essential diversity of visions and visionaries, we do not now contradict ourselves by presenting *our vision*, single, authoritative, comprehensive and final! Rather, we have given hints and put forward theses.

We go on now to offer half a dozen glimpses of what vision-forming in action can look like; we do so by looking at some actual current developments which bear the marks of vision. In their concreteness they should put some flesh on the bones of the more abstract theses.

We emphasise that in recounting them we are not holding them up as models to be imitated or parts to be put together into a composite whole or as in any way definitive or normative. The whole tenor of what we have said about the transcendent elusive-ness of vision and the essential diversity of visionaries will have made clear that we are counselling against blueprints and warning against imitation.

What follows are evocative – and provocative – stories, which may give glimpses or echoes of a vision and so may stimulate readers to be more visionary in their own, possibly very different situations. These may also illustrate the ambiguity of all such inno-vative and imaginative endeavours, in the mixture of motives, the mix of success and failure, the trade-offs with losses accompanying gains, and the unforeseen and unintended consequences of actions.

Also implicit in our choice is that vision-forming is not an activity in an armchair in advance of action; it is a form of action-reflection, in which the two elements, reflection and action, are to one another as chicken and egg.

Some Glimpses

1. *The European Union as Partnership*

We choose the idea of 'partnership' as a mode of governance in the European Union (EU) as one of our glimpses for the follow-ing reasons. It expresses a particular way of dealing with some of the problems that we encounter within the context of the EU. The problem here has been that the EU has been seen by many as marking the beginning of a European super state; one that takes governance and decisionmaking even further away from the mass of people. One of the counters to that has been the notion of sub-sidiarity, which, borrowed from Aristotle, can be seen as part of Catholic social doctrine. This places governance and decision making at the most appropriate lowest level, thus contributing to the break up of the nation state and to an increasing emphasis upon the sub-national level; a form of 'co-operative regionalism'. Thus, institutions like the Committee of the Regions help to strengthen the regional and local level and at the same time promote the breaking down of state-like hierarchical structures. But this is not the whole story. It must be remembered that 'the most appropriate lowest level' means just that and therefore it might mean the highest level, Brussels, or some intermediate level. It is the interaction and partnership between these levels that might be seen as the linking of local expressions of will with the more universal planning needs. Thus something like the BSE crisis needs sanction at national level. It also clearly needs a Community wide plan co-ordinating and dealing with the various national interests involved which would be inappropriate were it dealt with just at UK level. At the same time it needs to deal with various local levels both at the UK central government level, which has to deal with national food policy, and also with more regional levels, the situation and the problems in Scotland and Northern Ireland, for example.

We do not want to make these glimpses wholly positive, in the sense that they show a clear blueprint for the way forward. That would be against the point of a book that stresses the faith and hope involved in making leaps and not knowing the fullness of the destination. The possibilities of error and failure are built in and we must not discount them to construct a world free of those possibilities – for that, on our reading of it, would be the true failure. The example we choose exemplifies both how things can go forward but also the fragility of the way forward in showing the subversions of that way. Thus subsidiarity is highjacked by the UK government as a reaffirmation of British sovereignty instead of an attack on all sovereignties.

Subsidiarity, in the context of the EU, has been divided by some into two conceptions. First, procedural subsidiarity, which, though it devolves the site of decision making, does not necessarily make decision making local. The Scottish Office, where decisions are taken locally but by the UK central government, is a good example. Second, substantive subsidiarity, which would mean that decision making is actually taken by the local level. These can become coupled. Certain powers can be transferred to lower tiers of government and become the responsibility of local actors or perhaps be shared between different tiers. An excellent example of this is the implementation of the EU Structural Funds. Here it is widely recognised that local actors should be involved in a policy process that was designed to impact upon local economies (more than economies, lives and lifestyles). In the UK this has perhaps not been quite so clear and we go on to look at the example of the Highlands and Islands.

Since 1988 it has been an explicit requirement that access to the funds is on condition that regions, in conjunction with national governments and 'social partners' (industry and labour) submit regional development plans to the Commission, detailing the arrangements for the spending of such funds. Partnership in the context of the Community structural funds has been called by Bruce Millan, 'close involvement of regional and local bodies with the Commission and national authorities in planning and implementing development measures'. What is required in this concept is that Community operations be established through close consultation between the Commission and member states concerned. This includes other appropriate bodies, the partners, at national, local and regional level.

In 1994 a programme for Community structural assistance was developed by the UK government. Among other criteria this was placed within the framework of partnership. What does this mean in the context of Highland and Islands development? One of the ways it is institutionally expressed is by the Highlands and Islands monitoring committee. This is in its nature indeterminate since the committees are composed at national level and thus their composition will be determined by a mixture of the law and custom of that particular country. Thus this particular committee consists of members from the local authorities, the Highlands and Islands Enterprise network, the Scottish Office, Scottish National Heritage, the Scottish Tourist Board, the voluntary sector, the commercial sector and the further education sector. At the same time the decision was taken to encourage the formation of more locally based partnership groups, informal in nature, whose views would be taken into account when considering application for funds from particular areas.

Joanne Scott, to whom we are indebted for the material here, has written a lengthy description and critique of it viewed as a way of furthering participation, responsiveness and new forms of governance. In part this may be viewed as saying that this is not, in practice, a glimpse of the way forward. The new procedure is characterised by a lack of transparency; the local partnership groups are not to be represented upon the monitoring committee and ultimately it appears that it is there (and to a lesser extent in the advisory groups) that the power will be vested. The criteria for vetting projects will be essentially mechanical and thus in general the dialogue and exchange between local groups and regional, and higher level, sectors will not readily be facilitated. One can see both the possibilities and the limitations. The recognition that membership of the committee should extend beyond those directly elected recognises the necessity of facilitating greater, and more diverse, forms of participation than those provided for by representative democracy. Extending the partnership groups into the local areas brings the decision making closer to people. Yet at the same time we can see the limitations. The deliberations are in secret and the whole system of going down into the local could also smack of 'quangocracy', a new version of corporatism.

However within this are, as we have shown, possibilities that do show a way forward, and which point to at least a glimpse of a different future in organisation of governance. Subsidiarity might be deployed in a way that manages the ever increasing diversity in the EU and at the same time retain some sort of universalism, or, to put it in economic terms, manage the increasing diversity with the EU in such a way that it is no threat to economic and political integration. We can see these trends in what we have described. Subsidiarity requires decisions to be made at the closest level possible to the citizen. Failure to observe this might interfere with further integration. Citizens might prefer imperfect though generally understood domestic decision making procedures to less imperfect decision making procedures at the level of the EU – they prefer, as Charles Taylor points out, participation. This might require a system of co-operative regionalism whereby autonomous regions acquire increasing powers to shape EU policies. In a situation where regions have a greater role to play, then the principle of substantive subsidiarity will be more observed. Thus again, there might be a process of reciprocal feedback that would strengthen this trend, and, this trend would extend down into the localities as well. In this way then, we can integrate the local and the national, democracy and rationality, law and love.

2. The Assynt Crofters

Assynt can seem to be on the margins, a long way from where the 'real' life of Scotland is happening, yet the successful struggle of the crofters there to buy their land was as much about local people getting together to win some control of the future of their community as many of the struggles going on in the Urban Priority Areas of the Central belt.

The spectacular landscape of Assynt still carries signs of the clearances, and that history is very much part of a powerful folk memory which formed one dimension of the struggle. The more recent history of the North Lochinver estate was of ownership by one of the richest families in the UK, who remain the major landowners in Assynt; in 1989, the estate (some 9500 hectares) was bought by a Swedish property company, which went bankrupt in 1992. When the liquidators put the estate on the market again, advertising it as a place 'where people are perhaps alien' (despite the presence of several hundred crofting tenants), and with the alarming prospect for the crofters of it being further subdivided into seven parcels of land, the Assynt Crofters Trust was formed with the aim of raising funds to buy the estate and manage it on behalf of the crofters – an option which would retain the crofting tenancies of the individual crofters but give them the security of joint control over sensitive issues of development in their unique corner of Scotland.

The campaign captured public imagination, newspaper headlines and some powerful support; no doubt there were echoes in some urban minds of the spirit of such Scottish films as *Whisky Galore*. The crofters were a determined mix of families with roots in the area going back generations and relatively recent incomers equally committed to the crofting way of life, with feet firmly planted on solid ground and a clear, shared vision at least of immediate objectives. As in the groups in Easterhouse, there was no conventionally political agenda – neither explicit nor hidden – but a passionate commitment to a community.

The thrill of their victory in February 1993 was shared by many in a nation proud of an instinctive support for the underdog, but was greatest in Assynt where the celebratory ceilidh was much more than a media event. Yet, a few years on, Assynt north of Lochinver looks not much different from Assynt south of Lochinver (still owned by a traditional 'laird' absent for much of the year); at a first glance from the tourist, the revolution does not seem to have happened.

Quietly, however, and working as a community, the Assynt Crofters Trust has done much to improve both the social and environmental dimensions of the community. The crofters have enjoyed the steep learning curve of the past few years, proud to take on responsibility for their own progress while recognising their need for assistance from other agencies. Like groups in Easterhouse, they have learned to put together funding packages for projects such as that of planting native woodland (over 160 hectares already) which will not only enhance the environment sympathetically but generate local employment. In partnership with outside bodies, they have put together a Young Entrants Scheme which has already encouraged new young crofters into tenancies; a housing needs survey has been prepared with a view to ensuring the affordable housing needed to help young people stay in the area; funding has been secured for a project on crofting tourism; a hydro scheme which might sell electricity to the National Grid is at an early stage; and they are participating in the trans-European STEM project on computer-based land management.

An international company, by virtue of modern technology, carries on its business from the estate house undeterred by the occasional blocking of the single-track road outside by some large pigs. There are one or two small tourist-oriented developments, some better fencing to keep sheep off the road, and an active local history society. While not primarily oriented toward environmental issues, the Trust is recognised as demonstrating an awareness of the need for environmentally sensitive use of the estate's natural resources.

Beyond Assynt, the crofters' initiative has been inspirational for other groups which have tried to go down the same route with varying degrees of success; some of their projects also carry vital lessons for other communities. Yet the relative novelty of the Trust also brings problems, not least in that some agencies remain strangers to the idea of developing local community skills rather than using external expertise. European support for particular projects, particularly in the absence of a 'hands-on' rural development extension service, has been vital.

Crofting remains what it has long been, hard work for little reward, which has to be combined with other jobs in tourism or whatever in order to make a standard of living which by material standards of anywhere else in the country would be reckoned deprived. But real changes are taking place. Crucially, the pace of development is community determined, and a rich variety of people are finding ways of participating, not always in the idyllic peace that Assynt conveys to the tourist but creatively managing to pull together. Scratch the surface and one can find tensions and problems, as elsewhere; but, scratching the surface of the initial euphoria of the Assynt Crofters' victory, one finds an ongoing story of steady achievement both material and spiritual, and another glimpse of a possible future.

3. Community Groups in Easterhouse

A couple of days spent in Easterhouse (the second happening in the wake of the media hype surrounding a visit by President Chirac and Prince Charles) seems a scant basis to pontificate on anything, and close to a caricature of what makes folk in the community resentful of generalisations by outsiders. Yet the opportunity to interview some people involved in various community groups was immensely encouraging, as a brief encounter with a community bustling with a range of action groups, support groups *etc*, which are lively enough to have a culture of their own. Through the experience of listening to the excitement, sense of achievement and commitment of an overlapping network of people both volunteers and employees of funded projects, there was a definite sense of a community trying to reshape itself.

That is not to deny that there are the frustrations, jealousies and divisions very familiar to anyone involved with such groups in any community. But the overwhelming sense of listening to these community activists as a stranger was of encouragement; perhaps the downside of the groups in one's own community is more apparent with greater involvement and familiarity, but perhaps also one misses some vital dimensions of the positive looking more from the inside (the wood becoming invisible among the trees).

Arriving with an agenda about 'vision', we quickly became aware that our language of vision was largely a foreign one – not primarily because our words are academic, but because vision is not a natural part of how these community activists think or talk. These are not people who have caught hold of a vision and got involved in community action because of that vision. Although there are certainly ingredients for a community vision in how they see the aims of their work (always highly concrete, in terms of better housing, health, even a Disney-style theme park providing local employment), any attempt to construct a coherent or inspirational social vision would inevitably be highly artificial – imposing a pattern that is not genuinely there.

Their relationship or attitude to 'politics' varied from the deeply involved to the cynicism of 'a plague on all their houses', though all were suspicious of conventional political parties and politicians. One could say that here was living proof of the end of socialism. Hardly anyone talked in traditional socialist terms, yet these were surely many of the folk who, two generations ago, would have been the key activists of the Labour movement. For those who are unemployed, trade unions seem irrelevant, and the professionalism of New Labour may discourage participation.

For most, the starting point lay in a sense of felt injustice (experienced personally or seen in others), leading to a determination to do something about that situation. People get involved in particular situations they care about. Often that involvement led on beyond a single issue to others, or to some broader groups, but there was still a (learned) suspicion of grand schemes and packages of answers, especially when these were seen to come from outside. People talked of their motivation in terms of caring and of enjoying helping people. Explicitly or implicitly, there are elements of Christian and of socialist traditions involved here, but not in terms of wide-scale visions.

The crucial factor (again not often explicit, but genuinely there) is hope. What keeps some people involved in frustrations of community groups is a sense of injustice coupled with a sense that changes must and can be achieved. Hope may not be there at the beginning but grows through involvement. This, for the folk we spoke to, was far from naive idealism, but hope translated into commitment and sustained via togetherness, small victories and many frustrations. Also crucial is a sense of community in what these groups with their overlapping memberships and activities are doing; the support of that interlinking and mutual respect (despite some rivalries and jealousies) are vital to sustaining their efforts, not least in overcoming low self-esteem and intimidation by authority. Another animating factor is a sense of seeking control of their own life as a community, resistance to outside criticism and solutions, and a pride in what can be done together.

In short, people respond to injustice by getting together to make things better; they have learned a suspicion of grandiose visions but are animated by realistic and defiant hopes. Justice, as redressing wrongs, is important but theories of justice are not. Democracy, in terms of people controlling their own lives and destinies in the community, is also a key factor, though not articulated in traditional terms; perhaps subsidiarity may be lurking here. That leaves open the question of whether any attempt to draw out some shared vision (as the early socialists did) would add to the undoubted community-building that is going on both in their achievements and in the process of getting there; attempting to impose one would be disastrous.

Liberation theologians would suggest that social visions arise in the context of struggles; those that are imposed from outside are utopian in the negative sense of lacking any realistic relationship to what is actually going on. Does that mean that such visions are more limited in horizon, and less radical, than the academic perspective which can afford to look to a different 'system' rather than nudging the present one into overcoming particular injustices for the sake of folk in pressing need? Not necessarily so; without idealising 'the poor' or their poverty, there are important things happening here. Of course, such community groups, and the 'community development' banner under which they often appear, are not the effective remedy for deep-seated poverty and continuing deprivation. Indeed, they may sometimes offer politicians a cheap alternative to radical economic change. But there is here resistance among those 'repressed' (Baumann's contrast with those 'seduced' by market society), a resistance that goes beyond the seduction of what is on offer which they have not. There are fragments of a vision being forged and genuine contempt for much of the fashionable talk of 'community'; perhaps more important, people are getting together to help one another and to overturn injustices. There is hope.

4. Credit Unions

Unlike the previous two 'glimpses' this is not a glimpse of one particular community, but of a dimension in the life of several communities, less common as yet in Scotland than in Northern Ireland, but growing in a climate where debt problems are rife and credit markets are lively. In a society where a piece of plastic offers 'Access' to all sorts of goodies, an increasingly free and apparently competitive credit market works in fact as two credit markets – a wide choice for those who have some security to offer, and who generally use credit for luxuries, and a more restricted and expensive market for those who have little security and who use credit for necessities. Many of the latter become trapped in a spiral of debt from which there seems no hope of escape, and there is urgent need to find ways of providing cheap, accessible credit to allow those who are struggling with daily expenditure to cope with sudden large expenses.

This is the background to the growth of credit unions, partially filling the gap in the credit market created by the withdrawal of such as the Trustee Savings Bank from their traditional role in providing a facility for the small saver and borrower. Indeed, the roots of the credit union movement have much in common with those a century and more ago of both Trustee Savings Banks and Building Societies. A group of people, united by a 'common bond' required by law, can form a credit union according to a strictly defined legal framework (a process for which support is usually available from local authorities). The 'common bond' may be anything from membership of a church or trade union, to sharing the same employer or living in a particular community.

There are clear drawbacks. The complexity of the system and need for elements of expertise often not obvious in a community provide a substantial deterrent, and the legal requirement that only those who are saving members of the union can borrow from it restricts its effectiveness in dealing with poverty. Yet the achievements of credit unions, particularly in areas of deprivation are considerable. Common bonds are strengthened; trust in one another, and the community's trust in itself, grow; expertise is built up through training and shared experience; and people feel that they have regained some measure of control over a problematic area of their lives. This is an area in which churches can play (and are playing) a vital role, offering sometimes access to expertise and the initial credibility and trust required to get things started; the areas where credit unions have flourished are by and large those where churches have taken a proactive role.

The credit union movement represents one response to the hopelessness of spiralling debt; it represents a shared resistance to the way in which the credit market operates to exploit those most vulnerable; and it represents a limited but practicable way of making things better, from the bottom up.

5. The Wise Group

The Wise Group, started in Glasgow 13 years ago in 1984 and now operating also in Lanarkshire, Ross and Cromarty, East London, Derby, Bolton and Sunderland, is a non-profitmaking enterprise which fulfils simultaneously two functions; it helps long-term unemployed people into long-term employment and it provides locally needed goods and services. It thus gives at one and the same time a service to the unemployed and a service to the neighbourhood.

There are four combined elements in what those who have long been unemployed receive, namely training, work experience, guidance in the search for long-term employment and a wage at the going rate. The services provided directly to the community so far have been mainly in four areas, namely environmental improvement ('Landwise' and 'Treewise'), house improvement in the form of heat insulation and security measures ('Heatwise'), recycling ('Wise Recycling') and care in the community.

This is an enterprise which has grown to substantial proportions, with an annual turnover now of nearly £14 million, with around 550 'trainee workers' at any one time (and over 5000 since its inception) and with a permanent staff of around 700, so that it is now one of the largest Glasgow-based employers. It has been successful in getting long-term unemployed people into long-term employment, which it regards as its primary purpose, with a success rate of between a half and two-thirds of the intake finding and keeping employment; this is remarkable given that around 40 per cent of those taken on had been out of work for two or more years. The quality both of the service to the trainee workers and of the service by them to the local communities is widely attested. Funding comes principally from public sources, local, national and European, though there is also some money from the private sector and approximately a quarter of the present income is earned from the services provided to the community. What does this enterprise illustrate and what lessons are to be learned from it?

Perhaps above all it illustrates our view that it is helpful to combine different sectors or approaches which are often kept separate either for ideological reasons or just out of habit. One could also describe this as a blurring of boundaries. The 'intermediate labour market', which the Wise Group illustrates, is a good example of such mixing of the categories or blurring of the boundaries. For one thing, it blurs the boundary between 'in work' and 'out of work'. The conventional wisdom is that one is either in work and therefore not on benefit or on benefit and therefore not permitted to work. By combining training, actual work and payment of the going rate for the job, this unhelpful division is overcome. It shows that one can be productive at the same time as one is preparing to be productive, and it throws out the hint that if one can be working while learning, one could also be learning while working.

Second, by being a 'partnership', this enterprise produces two kinds of combination or mix, a 'horizontal' mix of the public, private and voluntary sectors and a 'vertical' mix of local, national and European resources. It shows how a voluntary initiative can evoke cooperation from public and private institutions and how the strengths of the three sectors, voluntary, private and public can be effectively combined. It also shows in two ways how there can be effective cooperation between different geographical levels, local, national and transnational. First of all, the three political levels are all involved in funding; but second, what began as a local (Glasgow) initiative has been expanded in the direction of a national endeavour, both by its amoeba-like reproduction in other areas of the country and by the possibility of its being given the blessing of national government and adopted as part of macro public policy.

It illustrates a number of other things. One is that the profit-driven market economy requires to be assisted or complemented by non-profit-based social intervention, if certain needs are to be met. Two kinds of unmet need are met in some measure by the Wise Group type of effort, namely on the one hand the actualising of the labour potential of an unutilised part of the labour force and on the other hand some housing, environmental and other needs of local communities.

The Wise Group also illustrates the importance of close consultation between providers and receivers of services. It is not primarily a community development organisation; it did not start with a local community asking itself what its needs were; it started with an attempt to get long-term unemployed into employment. However, the local communities served have had a large say in the decisions about what should be provided. This has been specially true in the work of environmental improvement. The nature of the housing improvement tended to be more self-evident, though the inevitably disruptive process of improvement was a matter of close consultation.

This enterprise also shows that there is no reason why charitable, in the sense of non-profit-making enterprise, with socially 'worthy' aims need be 'amateurish' or less than professional and efficient. Reference has already been made to the high quality of the operations, with levels of supervision and management that benefit both the trainee workers and the communities served. This is a further aspect of the lesson which the Wise Group offers that 'real work' in the sense of the production of something of value is not necessarily confined to a context in which the provider makes a profit or the recipient has purchasing power.

6. The Camphill Communities

The Camphill Communities with people in need of special care offer us another practical example of how structured generosity might be accomplished. Founded in a borrowed manse in Aberdeen in 1940 by refugees from Nazism, these Communities were a practical, explicit and Christian reply to the programmes of 'euthanasia' of people with learning difficulties developed in Germany from 1933, and less explicitly, a reply to the incarceration of such people in British asylums. Currently there are 41 Camphill Communities in Britain and Ireland with a similar number in the rest of the world and a particular, growing presence in the former Soviet bloc as they try to help repair some of the damage done to those with learning difficulties by the former regimes.

Four features of the Camphill Communities are relevant for present purposes. First, there is the belief that behind the 'veil of handicap' there lies, in the person with learning difficulties, an undamaged human soul undiminished in its capacity for growth and development. It is this undamaged essence which is consistently addressed in the therapeutic work of the Communities and, unsurprisingly, they are often used as services of last resort by education and social work authorities unable to find other services willing to take on people with the most difficult and enigmatic difficulties. In comparison with, for example, behavioural approaches to learning difficulties, 'success' in these terms is not simply observable or measurable, and continuing care over years without the reassurance of such positive feedback represents a practical example of unconditional love for the other.

Second, the Communities show how the transformative power of love may become institutionalised, although they would correctly reject the negative connotations of this word. Rather than seeing those with learning difficulties in terms of a deficit model, people lacking in this, that or the other 'normal' attribute, the members of the Communities see the real difficulties of the other as a personal and communal challenge to understand and to change themselves. The difficulties of the other are seen as an exaggeration of traits present in everyone, difficulties which can only be encountered and eased if those trying to act therapeutically can recognise those traits and difficulties in themselves, addressing their own difficulties as a necessary pre-condition of trying to address the difficulties of the other.

An example might help: one of the authors, while researching the Communities, taught a class of 16-18 year olds for a period of a month. One of the members of this class was a young man with a severe endocrine disorder which resulted in behaviour which was often difficult to contain. One consequence of the disorder was a frequent drowsiness which, in class, resulted in naps, head on arms across the desk. Maintaining attention and time 'on task' was therefore a considerable pedagogic challenge, less so however than trying to deal with the minutes of whining self justification which resulted from the slightest challenge. With a rising tide of teacherly frustration, an impasse threatened. This was averted, and made productive, when the teacher's recognised his own tiredness and his envy of the pupil's feeling free to submit to tiredness, and also recognised his own tendency to self-justification and his dislike of this trait in himself as well as in the pupil.

Third, the Communities consciously eschew the wage relationship. Community members receive a small weekly personal needs (cigarette *etc*) allowance, other needs being met from resources held in common. The wage relationship is rejected for two inter-locking reasons: first therapeutic work with people with major learning difficulties depends, as described above, on the 'encounter of ego with ego', on the 'therapist' making contact with themselves and with the other at a deep level. Objectifying this relationship through concerns with issues of money and time would inhibit the encounter and militate against therapeutic work. The wage relationship is, second, rejected for reasons of social solidarity. Organising social relations around the individual wage (and its corollary, the family wage) atomises social relations and makes the use of resources for collective purposes appear an imposition on the individual. Holding resources collectively thus demands that individuals think about what their real needs are, about what the needs of others are, about how these might be balanced and it demands that an explicit consensus is reached about what collective needs are to be defined, balanced and met.

Finally, the Communities value people with learning difficulties as representing a continuing foil for seeing the nature of existing social relations more clearly. This is not in terms of any debate about the level of material care and support (what the taxpayer can afford) but in terms of the very difference of people with learning difficulties: the person who is slow in interpersonal interaction questions why we value a certain quick-wittedness; the person who distances themselves from interpersonal contact questions the distance we assume between us; the person who can produce only slowly questions why we value production for profit. Our acts of separating off and classifying this group as different tell us about our assumptions about normality and the values underpinning this. People with learning difficulties present an immanent critique of our existing social relations and can help point the way to different values and different social forms.

In none of these four aspects are the Camphill Communities perfect models of new social relations: the attempt to address the undamaged person behind the veil of handicap can lead to patronising claims of a superior knowledge; the search for reciprocal personal development can turn into an epicure-like valuing of the person with learning difficulties for what they developmental delights they offer to the therapist; the attempt to meet needs rather than pay wages can concentrate economic power in a non-transparent manner; seeing those with learning difficulties as an existential challenge to existing social relations can stereotype people with learning difficulties. However, as Nils Christie suggests, the Camphill Communities are places where new social forms are being, often painfully, explored. Starting from the attempt to offer unconditional love to people with significant personal difficulties collective structures are developing in the Communities which not only enable this love at a personal level but which build generosity into economic and social structures.

Discerning Coherence

These six accounts may give the impression that the outcome of this book is nothing more than a sequence of small, local fragments. We make no apology for dealing with what is small scale and localised and therefore fragmentary; indeed it is part of our message that such concreteness is too often avoided. However, we would reject any charge that we are offering 'nothing more' than that. We have spoken of discovering the unity in the diversity. In the six accounts which we have just given – from 'the encounter of ego with ego' of 'therapist' and 'therapee' in experimental communities, through the creation of new financial, business and community structures to counter directly experienced threats to individual and collective well-being, to the attempt to create governmental structures which can both unite traditionally hostile nation states and locate control in the most local level – there runs a common thread: the attempt to create new forms of social relationships to remove barriers to individual and collective participation in the development of more generous social structures. Thus, in and through the many very different situations both within this country and across the world there are common features; vision formation involves discovering the common directions in which things *are moving* and in which they may be moved; it is a way of discerning coherence within the variety and even between contradictions. Two words may sum up the directions in which things are moving, namely 'innovation' and 'globalisation', and one phrase may express the direction in which things may *'be moved'*, namely 'multiple participation'.

First, innovation. There is continuing, continual and accelerating innovation, affecting what and how we produce, what and how we consume, how we communicate and how we organise. This innovation is ambiguous in that it is at one and the same time creative and destructive. Schumpeter spoke of capitalist development as 'creative destruction', but the term may be applied more generally to innovation, of which capitalism is one instance. In the present phase of innovation, the process has been writ large and accelerated, taking on global proportions and apocalyptic overtones. The task now as in the past is to enhance its creativeness and reduce its destructiveness, to 'accentuate the positive, eliminate the negative'. Some of the negative or destructive features at present are evident. For example, the global enterprises which engage in major innovation, by their powerful command of material resources and of human organisation, including their capacity to move resources and operations across the world, can undermine local and regional coherences and can create great inequalities of power, wealth, income and general access to resources. On the other hand, the innovation can generate opportunities of positive human development for all. In particular, the innovation in ways of communicating presents the ambiguity of creation and destruction, making possible both the enhancement and the reduction of freedom, both the inclusion and the exclusion of people.

Closely associated with the scale and pace of recent and current innovation in general and in communication in particular is what has begun to be called 'globalisation', the creation of a planetary society in the sense of a worldwide field of social interaction. Of the many implications of the advent of this 'one world', two stand out. One is the discovery of the finitude of the planet, the limitation of its resources; for paradoxically the innovation which has consumed vast resources has led by way of one world consciousness to the discovery of the possibility (and now near-reality) of their exhaustion. Another very different discovery through the advent of one world is of the reality of many worlds, the rich diversity of cultures, of 'worlds' of meaning and communities of belonging.

It is in this context of 'innovation' and 'globalisation' that the issue of 'multiple participation' comes sharply to the fore. There are two senses of 'being part' of a community, one more passive and the other more active. It is now increasingly recognised, as we have been making clear, that people are 'part of' many communities simultaneously, local, regional, national, continental, global, public sector, private sector, voluntary sector, *etc*. This makes nonsense of the old notion of a single sovereign community, whether nation or race or whatever. So there is in fact 'multiple participation' in the sense that every person is, in the passive meaning, *part* of many communities at the same time.

But if there is 'multiple participation' in that sense, there *can be* another kind of 'multiple participation', namely in the sense that people can be and should be, in the active meaning, *part* of each of the communities of which, in the passive meaning, they are part. To participate in this latter, active sense is to share in the communal responsibility of the community, be it local or global or in between, be it public or private or voluntary. Of course it includes sharing in the benefits; but it also involves sharing in the costs. It is to be part of the giving and the receiving, of the taking of decisions and the taking of the fruits of them; for responsibility goes with opportunity, opportunity with responsibility. As we have said, both innovation and globalisation are ambiguous; part of their ambiguity is that they can reduce participation and so exclude people; but they also offer ways of increasing participation and so including people, presenting new opportunities of direct and active involvement by the many, in governments, in enterprises and in associations, and with the new means of communication dissolving distances. This 'multiple participation' is not only participation *within* these many communities; it is also participation *between* them. The one world which we seek is not the *single* sovereign state writ large; it is its antithesis; it is the interaction between *many* communities. It is such interactive participation that creates neighbours, as we have learned from the parable of the good Samaritan; and it is such neighbours who, to their surprise, see within the multiplicity an unlooked for coherence.

In Conclusion: Beyond Fear

'Acting in the middle' has been one of our key phrases. This is not to be confused with being 'middle of the road people', of whom it is said that they risk being knocked down by traffic from both directions, and who are derided as indeterminate and indecisive, derivative and uncreative. We hope that we have shown that to act in the middle in our sense is to be very active, decisive and creative, with the creativity that is radically transformative. It is to embrace uncertainty, no longer clinging to what is known but replacing the paralysing and deadening fear which seeks the safety of the known with the stimulating and enlivening anxiety which faces the risk of the unknown.

We are not speaking of the political Centre within a Left to Right spectrum: terms which in any case have become so ambiguous as to be unhelpful. We are speaking of acting in the middle firstly in relation to inherited traditions, notably those of socialism and of Christianity. We do so in the sense that we neither reject them, putting them in a historical dust bin, nor subordinate ourselves to them, placing them on a sacred pedestal. To treat any inherited tradition as dead is to be uncreatively haunted by it; to treat it as sacrosanct is to be uncreatively dominated by it. We try to do neither. Rather we engage with traditions and commend continuous engagement with them, knowing that in such engagement they are both developed and transcended (and whether their names survive becomes irrelevant).

Second, we commend acting in the middle between what *is* and what *can be*. We reject both what is commonly called 'realism' and what is commonly called 'idealism'. The so-called realism posits a reality in which we are embedded and by which we are bound, so that any change is merely an adjustment, adaptation or modification of what is, in a kind of rearrangement of the furniture. By contrast, the so-called idealism posits an ideal which is so disjoined from the real that it involves a flight from it, leaving the real unchanged and the ideal unrealised. As we have argued, both are devoid of hope and derive from fear. The hope that transcends fear leads us to act in the middle, which means acting on what *is* in such a way as to create out of it what yet transcends it and thus transforms it. This way of acting is that of self-transcending love, which creates law but is not reduced to it, which forms structures but does not become dependent on them, and which transforms both persons and politics.

Which brings us to a third sense of acting in the middle, that between persons and politics; this means that neither is absorbed in the other and neither is separated from the other; they are distinct but interactive, so that the most creative act is at once fully personal and fully political.

It is to such 'acting in the middle' that we invite our fellow citizens including our elected civil representatives, in Europe, in Britain, and in Scotland; it is an invitation to take up the cross, an invitation to a way of acting which involves individual people and whole communities in transcending fear, forming vision, acting hope and structuring generosity.

Having concluded with this invitation, we have come only to the end of the beginning.